THE LONG LAKE ANTHOLOGY OF POETS:
Stand Up Michael!

Compiled by Eddy Duhan
For Long Lake Publishing

ISBN 978-0982905944

All Material is Public Domain, except the original works from PD sources adapted by Eddy Duhan and by John Andrew Schreiner (from: 'The Odes of Solomon', and 'The Holy Bible')
"Besieged by Chinaski" adapted by Eddy Duhan from "Besieged" by Charles Bukowski

(Copyright 2012, Long Lake Publishing
Administered by
Lori Kelly Rights and Licenses, LKRL1@aol.com)
longlakemusic@yahoo.com

Acknowledgments and Inspiration: Jan and Sarah, John Andrew Schreiner, Chuck Fromm and Worship Leader Magazine (theodesproject.net), Wayne Zeitner, Charles Bukowski, Nik Venet, and Jesus Christ.

Cover photo: Michael casting Lucifer out of heaven.
Back cover photo: A 13th-century Byzantine icon St. Catherine's Monastery, Mount Sinai.
Poets photos from Google images.

Dedicated to Sarah

Introduction

This book is a compilation of works that are in the public domain from many of my favorite poets. I have chosen not to include any of their bios because I wanted the poetry to stand on its own; and most everyone knows who they are. If not, you can Google their names and probably find volumes written about each one of them online and in print. I dedicate this book to my daughter Sarah, who I find is quite the little musical poet herself! One day she came home from school and told me how the maintenance worker put a tall ladder up against a building to get to the roof and how the sun seemed to be sitting just above the top rung. She wrote this song from the inspiration and performed it for her church choir:

Ladder to the Light
High, medium, low wanna live a pure life or a sinful one,
how big is your ladder? High, medium, or low--------------.
If you wanna get to the light you gotta make it
a little Higher, little higher, little higher then---- you'll be with the Lord!

So may *you* climb up close to the Lord with childlike faith! And have *peace* and *unity* with God, the Great Bible Poet Himself, through Jesus Christ our Lord, who with a word brought everything into existence, and with a word holds everything together! *"Colossians 1:**12** Giving thanks unto the Father, which hath made us meet to be partakers of the inheritance of the saints in light: **13** Who hath delivered us from the power of darkness, and hath translated us into the kingdom of his dear Son: **14** In whom we have redemption through his blood, even the forgiveness of sins: **15** Who is the image of the invisible God, the firstborn of every creature: **16** For by him were all things created , that are in heaven, and that are in earth, visible and* *invisible, whether they be thrones, or dominions, or principalities, or powers: all things were created by him, and for him:* **17** *And he is before all things, and by him all things consist."*

So what is this life and universe anyway? An energy force of compressed atoms; shaped into form by a word from God's mouth? He said: "Let ther be…" and it was! Is it a cosmic contest between the children of the devil and the children of God, intertwined in a battle between good and evil? Is it an illusion, a dream? Where we are the dream, and God is the dreamer? Where the only concrete reality is the spiritual realm of eternity, light and love! *Eddy.*

CONTENTS

1. The Cursed Poets / 9

Hank Chinaski / 10
    1. Roll Over Chinaski / 11
    2. Besieged By Chinaski / 13
Charles Baudelaire / 14
    3. Poetry In Prose / 15
    4. Benediction / 17
Arthur Rimbaud / 20
    5. Poor People In Church / 21
    6. Farewell / 23

2. The Christian Poets / 25

William Blake / 26
    7. And Did Those Feet In Ancient Time / 27
    8. The Lamb / 28
    9. Night / 29
    10. The Tiger / 31
John Donne / 32
    11. Holy Sonnet 14 / 33
    12. A Hymn To God The Father / 34
John Milton / 35
    13. When He Fled From Absalom / 36
    14. Upon The Circumcision / 37
St. Frances / 38
    15. All Creatures Of Our God And King / 39
John Bunyan / 41
    16. A Boy And Watchmaker / 42
Methodius / 44
    17. The Virgin's Song / 45
Clement / 52
    18. Hymn To Christ / 53
T S Eliot / 55

    19. The Hippopotamus / 56
    20. 18. Little Gidding / 58
    21. Journey Of The Magi / 66
    22. The Wasteland / 68

Robert Service / 81
    23. The Call Of The Wild / 82
    24. Spell Of The Yukon / 84
    25. The Woman And The Angel / 87

Clive Hamilton(C.S. Lewis) / 89
    26. Spirits In Bondage / 90

Wordsworth / 134
    27. Gracious Spirit, Holy Ghost / 135
    28. O Lord of Heaven and Earth and Sea / 136
    29. Songs of Thankfulness and Praise / 137

Emily Dickinson / 138
    30. Tie the strings to my life, my Lord / 139
    31. The Chariot / 140
    32. Safe in their alabaster chambers / 141

3. The Musical Poets / 142

Sarah F. Adams / 143
    33. Nearer, My God, to Thee / 144

Fanny Crosby / 145
    34. Blessed Assurance / 146
    35. Holy, Holy, Holy Is The Lord / 147
    36. To God Be The Glory / 148

Charles Wesley / 149
    37. O For a Thousand Tongues to Sing / 150
    38. Jesus, Lover of My Soul / 153

John Newton / 154
    39. Amazing Grace / 155
    40. Approach, My Soul, the Mercy Seat / 156
    41. Dear Shepherd of thy People, Hear / 157
    42. How Sweet the Name of Jesus Sounds / 158

Ambrose of Milan / 159

    43. Now That the Daylight Fills the Sky / 160
    44. O Splendor of God's Glory Bright / 161
Ephrem the Syrian / 162
    45. Get Up My Soul Arise / 163
    46. I Run To You With Love / 164
James Weldon Johnston / 165
    47. Lift Ev'ry Voice and Sing / 166
    48. Go Down Death / 168
    49. Listen, Lord: A Prayer / 171
John Andrew Schreiner / 173
    50. Meditation On Paradise / 174
    51. I Have Been Freed / 175
    52. I Shall Not Fear / 177
    53. He Blesses His People With Peace / 178
    54. A Cloud Of Peace / 180
Eddy Duhan / 181
    55. Creation Song / 182
    56. I Will Wait For My Change To Come / 183
    57. Lamentation / 184
    58. Let Light Shine / 185
    59. Treasures In Heaven / 186
    60. Song Of Moses / 187
    61. Bible Prayers / 188
    62. The Lord Said To My Lord / 189
    63. Stand Up Michael / 190

1.
The Cursed Poets

Son of man, take up a lamentation upon the king of Tyrus, and say unto him, Thus saith the Lord GOD; Thou sealest up the sum, full of wisdom, and perfect in beauty.
Thou hast been in Eden the garden of God; every precious stone was thy covering, the sardius, topaz, and the diamond, the beryl, the onyx, and the jasper, the sapphire, the emerald, and the carbuncle, and gold: the workmanship of thy tabrets and of thy pipes was prepared in thee in the day that thou wast created.
Thou art the anointed cherub that covereth; and I have set thee so: thou wast upon the holy mountain of God; thou hast walked up and down in the midst of the stones of fire.
Thou wast perfect in thy ways from the day that thou wast created, till iniquity was found in thee.
By the multitude of thy merchandise they have filled the midst of thee with violence, and thou hast sinned: therefore I will cast thee as profane out of the mountain of God: and I will destroy thee, O covering cherub, from the midst of the stones of fire.
Thine heart was lifted up because of thy beauty, thou hast corrupted thy wisdom by reason of thy brightness: I will cast thee to the ground, I will lay thee before kings, that they may behold thee.
Thou hast defiled thy sanctuaries by the multitude of thine iniquities, by the iniquity of thy traffick; therefore will I bring forth a fire from the midst of thee, it shall devour thee, and I will bring thee to ashes upon the earth in the sight of all them that behold thee.
All they that know thee among the people shall be astonished at thee: thou shalt be a terror, and never shalt thou be any more.
Ezekiel 28.(KJV)

Henry Chinaski

"For those who believe in God, most of the big questions are answered. But for those of us who can't readily accept the God formula, the big answers don't remain stone-written. We adjust to new conditions and discoveries. We are pliable. Love need not be a command nor faith a dictum. I am my own god. We are here to unlearn the teachings of the church, state, and our educational system. "We are here to drink beer. We are here to kill war. We are here to laugh at the odds and live our lives so well that Death will tremble to take us"

Roll over Chinaski

Henry Chinaski
was the greatest loser
boozer poet
of all time

(he died 18 years ago;
to the day that Duhan published
"All Men Are Like Flies")

Chinaski
won't enter
the
public domain
until 2064.

too bad!
that means
I would have to
get someone's
permission
to include
his poems
in this book.

Ha! I could adapt
and rhyme one_
changing it just enough, maybe?

I'm sure
that would
make the Chinaski roll over
in his grave,

I could make up
"the lost Chinaski poem"
the one about how the government
passed a law
mandating that:
"every man woman and child
in America
be required
to buy
this poetry book
for the good health of
their souls…
and for the general insanity of the public!
and if they do not then
they will be fined
and disallowed
by the IRS!"

or, I could just try
to sneak
one of Hank's poems in unnoticed!
but then I would have trouble…
from the establishment,
and the Huntington Library,
and the black sparrow of death!

now look at what you've
done, Duhan!
you went and lumped
yourself
in with the
Cursed Poets!

Besieged by Chinaski

this wall is green
that wall is blue
these walls have ears
they have eyes too.

this wall frames my mother's face
this wall a sheet of frozen ice
the other wall is melting wax
my father's bones spill from the cracks.

outside is the city
more cruel than any walls
almost nothing is far better
than nothing at all.

never dare to venture out
disconnect the phone and lower the shades
it creeps to the call of bells and lights
the city is an open grave.

and the last wall will crawl
with angry famished spiders
finally the walls are all we have
to remain within and hide forever.

Charles Baudelaire

"There are in every man, at every hour, two simultaneous postulations, one towards God, the other towards Satan "

Prose in Poetry

grave, lost, as it is, in a Paradise shutting out all thought, of the grave and of destruction.

The whole audience, blase and frivolous as it was, soon fell under the all-powerful sway of the artist. Not a thought was left of death, of mourning, or of punishment.
All gave themselves up, without disquietude, to the manifold delights caused by the sight of a masterpiece of living art. Explosions of joy and admiration again and again shook the dome of the edifice with the energy of a continuous thunder. The Prince himself, in an ecstasy, joined in the applause of his court.

Nevertheless, to a discerning eye, his emotion was not unmixed. Did he feel himself conquered in his power as despot? humiliated in his art as the striker of terror into hearts, of chill into souls? Such suppositions, not exactly justified, but not absolutely unjustifiable, passed through my mind as I contemplated the face of the Prince, on which a new pallor gradually overspread its habitual paleness, as snow overspreads snow. His lips compressed themselves tighter and tighter, and his eyes lighted up with an inner fire like that of jealousy or of spite, even while he applauded the talents of his old friend, the strange buffoon, who played the buffoon so well in the face of death. At a certain moment, I saw his Highness lean towards a little page, stationed behind him, and whisper in his ear. The roguish face of the pretty child lit up with a smile, and he briskly quitted the Prince's box as if to execute some urgent commission.

A few minutes later a shrill and prolonged hiss interrupted Fancioulle in one of his finest moments, and rent alike every ear and heart. And from the part of the house from whence this unexpected note of disapproval had sounded, a child darted into a corridor with stifled laughter.

Benediction

When, by decree of the supreme power,
The Poet appears in this annoyed world,
His mother, blasphemous out of horror
At God's pity, cries out with fists curled:

"Ah! I'd rather You'd will me a snake's skin
Than to keep feeding this monstrous slur!
I curse that night's ephemera are sins
To make my womb atone for pleasure.

"Since You have chosen me from all the brides
To bear the disgust of my dolorous groom
And since I can't throw back into the fires
Like an old love letter this gaunt buffoon

"I'll replace Your hate that overwhelms me
On the instrument of Your wicked gloom
And torture so well this miserable tree
Its pestiferous buds will never bloom!"

She chokes down the eucharist of venom,
Not comprehending eternal designs,
She prepares a Gehenna of her own,
And consecrates a pyre of maternal crimes.

Yet, watched by an invisible seraph,
The disinherited child is drunk on the sun
And in all he devours and in all he quaffs
Receives ambrosia, nectar and honey.

He plays with the wind, chats with the vapors,
Deliriously sings the stations of the cross;
And the Spirit who follows him in his capers
Cries at his joy like a bird in the forest.

Those whom he longs to love look with disdain
And dread, strengthened by his tranquility,
They seek to make him complain of his pain
So they may try out their ferocity.

In the bread and wine destined for his lips,
They mix in cinders and spit with their wrath,
And throw out all he touches as he grasps it,
And accuse him of putting his feet in their path.

His wife cries out so that everyone hears:
"Since he finds me good enough to adore
I'll weave as the idols of ancient years
A corona of gold as a cover.

"I'll get drunk on nard, incense and myrrh,
Get down on bent knee with meats and wines
To see if in a heart that admires,
My smile denies deference to the divine.

"And, when I tire of these impious farces,
I'll arrange for him my frail and hard nails
Sharpened just like the claws of a harpy
That out of his heart will carve a trail.

"Like a baby bird trembling in the nest
I'll dig out his heart all red from my breast
To slake the thirst of my favorite pet,
And will throw it on the ground with contempt!"

Toward the sky, where he sees a great host,
The poet, serene, lifts his pious arms high
And the vast lightning of his lucid ghost
Blinds him to the furious people nearby:

"Glory to God, who leaves us to suffer

To cure us of all our impurities
And like the best, most rarefied buffer
Prepares the strong for a saint's ecstasies!

"I know that You hold a place for the Poet
In the ranks of the blessed and the saint's legions,
That You invite him to an eternal fete
Of thrones, of virtues, of dominations.

"I know only sorrow is unequaled,
It cannot be encroached on from Hell or Earth
And if I am to braid my mystic wreath,
May I impose it on the universe.

"But the ancient jewels of lost Palmyra,
The unknown metals, pearls from the ocean
By Your hand mounted, they do not suffice,
They cannot dazzle as clearly as this crown

"For it will not be made except from halos
Drawn of pure light in a holy portal
Whose entire splendor, in the eyes of mortals
Is only a mirror, obscure and mournful."

Arthur Rimbaud

"I believe I am in Hell, therefore I am."

Poor People in Church

between oaken pews,
in corners of the church which their breath stinkingly warms,
all their eyes on the chancel dripping with gold,
and the choir with its twenty pairs of jaws bawling pious hymns;

Sniffing the odour of wax if it were the odour of bread,
happy, ad humbled like beaten dogs,
the Poor offer up to God, the Lord and Master,
their ridiculous stubborn oremuses.

For the women it is very pleasant to wear the benches smooth;
after the six black days on which God has made them suffer.
They nurse, swaddled in strange-looking shawls,
creatures like children who weep as if they would die.

Their unwashed breasts hanging out, these eaters of soup,
with a prayer in their eyes, but never praying,
watch a group of hoydens wickedly
showing off with hats all out of shape.

Outside is the cold, and hunger - and a man on the booze.
All right. There's another hour to go; afterwards, nameless ills! -
Meanwhile all around an assortment of old
dewlapped women whimpers, snuffles, and whispers:

These are distracted persons and the epileptics from whom,
yesterday, you turned away at street crossings;
there too are the blind who are led by a dog into courtyards,
poring their noses into old-fashioned missals. –

And all of them, dribbling a stupid groveling faith,
recite their unending complaint to Jesus who is dreaming
up there,
yellow from the livid stained glass window,
far above thin rascals and wicked potbellies,
far from the smell of meat and mouldy fabric,
and the exhausted somber farce of repulsive gestures -
and as the prayer flowers in choice expressions,
and the mysteries take on more emphatic tones, from the
aisles,
where the sun is dying, trite folds of silk and green smiles,
the ladies of the better quarters of the town - oh Jesus! -
the sufferers from complaints of the liver,
make their long yellow fingers kiss the holy water in the
stoups.

Farewell

Autumn already!... But why regret the everlasting sun, if we are sworn to a search for divine brightness-- far from those who die as seasons turn.... Autumn. Our boat, risen out of a hanging fog, turns toward poverty's harbor, the monstrous city, its sky stained with fire and mud. Ah! Those stinking rags, bread soaked with rain, drunkenness, and the thousands of loves who nailed me to the cross! Will there never, ever be an end to that ghoulish queen of a million dead souls and bodies and who will all be judged!, I can see myself again, my skin corroded by dirt and disease, hair and armpits crawling with worms, and worms still larger crawling in my heart, stretched out among ageless, heartless, unknown figures.... I could easily have died there.... What a horrible memory! I detest poverty. And I dread winter because it's so cozy!

--Sometimes in the sky I see endless sandy shores covered with white rejoicing nations. A great golden ship, above me, flutters many-colored pennants in the morning breeze. I was the creator of every feast, every triumph, every drama. I tried to invent new flowers, new planets, new flesh, new languages. I thought I had acquired supernatural powers. Ha! I have to bury my imagination and my memories! What an end to a splendid career as an artist and storyteller! I! I called myself a magician, an angel, free from all moral constraint.... I am sent back to the soil to seek some obligation, to wrap gnarled reality in my arms. A peasant! Am I deceived? Would Charity be the sister of death, for me?

Well, I shall ask forgiveness for having lived on lies. And that's that. But not one friendly hand... and where can I look for help? True; the new era is nothing if not harsh. For I can say that I have gained a victory; the gnashing of teeth, the hissing of hellfire, the stinking sighs subside. All my monstrous memories are fading. My last longings depart-- jealousy of beggars, bandits, friends of death, all those that the world passed by-- Damned souls, if I were to take vengeance! One must be absolutely modern. Never mind hymns of thanksgiving: hold on to a step once taken. A hard night! Dried blood smokes on my face, and nothing lies behind me but that repulsive little tree! The battle for the soul is as brutal as the battles of men; but the sight of justice is the pleasure of God alone.

Yet this is the watch by night. Let us all accept new strength, and real tenderness. And at dawn, armed with glowing patience, we will enter the cities of glory. Why did I talk about a friendly hand! My great advantage is that I can laugh at old love affairs full of falsehood, and stamp with shame such deceitful couples-- I went through women's Hell over there-- and I will be able now to possess the truth within one body and one soul.

2.

The Christian Poets

33Who through faith subdued kingdoms, wrought righteousness, obtained promises, stopped the mouths of lions. 34Quenched the violence of fire, escaped the edge of the sword, out of weakness were made strong, waxed valiant in fight, turned to flight the armies of the aliens. 35Women received their dead raised to life again: and others were tortured, not accepting deliverance; that they might obtain a better resurrection: 36And others had trial of cruel mockings and scourgings, yea, moreover of bonds and imprisonment: 37They were stoned, they were sawn asunder, were tempted, were slain with the sword: they wandered about in sheepskins and goatskins; being destitute, afflicted, tormented; 38(Of whom the world was not worthy:) they wandered in deserts, and in mountains, and in dens and caves of the earth. 39And these all, having obtained a good report through faith, received not the promise: 40God having provided some better thing for us, that they without us should not be made perfect. Hebrews 11 (KJV)

William Blake

"It is not because angels are holier than men or devils that makes them angels, but because they do not expect holiness from one another, but from God only."

And Did those Feet in Ancient Time

And did those feet in ancient time,
Walk upon England's mountains green:
And was the holy Lamb of God,
On England's pleasant pastures seen?
And did the Countenance Divine,
Shine forth upon our clouded hills?
And was Jerusalem builded here,
Among these dark Satanic Mills?
Bring me my Bow of burning gold:
Bring me my Arrows of desire:
Bring me my Spear: O clouds unfold!
Bring me my Chariot of fire!
I will not cease from Mental Fight,
Nor shall my Sword sleep in my hand:
Till we have built Jerusalem,
In England's green and pleasant Land.

The Lamb

    Little Lamb, who made thee
        Dost thou know who made thee,
Gave thee life, and bid thee feed
By the stream and o'er the mead;
Gave thee clothing of delight,
Softest clothing, woolly, bright;
Gave thee such a tender voice,
Making all the vales rejoice?
    Little Lamb, who made thee?
    Dost thou know who made thee?
    Little Lamb, I'll tell thee;
    Little Lamb, I'll tell thee:
He is called by thy name,
For He calls Himself a Lamb
He is meek, and He is mild,
He became a little child.
I a child, and thou a lamb,
We are called by His name.
    Little Lamb, God bless thee!
    Little Lamb, God bless thee!

Night

The sun descending in the west,
The evening star does shine;
The birds are silent in their nest,
And I must seek for mine.
    The moon, like a flower
    In heaven's high bower,
    With silent delight,
    Sits and smiles on the night.
Farewell, green fields and happy grove,
Where flocks have ta'en delight.
Where lambs have nibbled, silent move
The feet of angels bright;
    Unseen they pour blessing,
    And joy without ceasing,
    On each bud and blossom,
    And each sleeping bosom.
They look in every thoughtless nest
Where birds are covered warm;
They visit caves of every beast,
To keep them all from harm:
    If they see any weeping
    That should have been sleeping,
    They pour sleep on their head,
    And sit down by their bed.
When wolves and tigers howl for prey,
They pitying stand and weep;
Seeking to drive their thirst away,
And keep them from the sheep.
    But, if they rush dreadful,
    The angels, most heedful,
    Receive each mild spirit,
    New worlds to inherit.
And there the lion's ruddy eyes
Shall flow with tears of gold:

And pitying the tender cries,
And walking round the fold:
    Saying: "Wrath by His meekness,
    And, by His health, sickness,
    Are driven away
    From our immortal day.
"And now beside thee, bleating lamb,
I can lie down and sleep,
Or think on Him who bore thy name,
Graze after thee, and weep.
    For, washed in life's river,
    My bright mane for ever
    Shall shine like the gold,
    As I guard o'er the fold."

The Tiger

Tiger, tiger, burning bright
In the forests of the night,
What immortal hand or eye
Could frame thy fearful symmetry?
In what distant deeps or skies
Burnt the fire of thine eyes?
On what wings dare he aspire?
What the hand dare seize the fire?

And what shoulder and what art
Could twist the sinews of thy heart?
And when thy heart began to beat,
What dread hand and what dread feet?
What the hammer? what the chain?
In what furnace was thy brain?
What the anvil? What dread grasp
Dare its deadly terrors clasp?

John Donne

"Any man's death diminishes me, because I am involved in Mankind; And therefore never send to know for whom the bell tolls; it tolls for thee."

Holy Sonnet 14

Batter my heart, three-personed God, for you
As yet but knock, breathe, shine, and seek to mend;
That I may rise, and stand, o'erthrow me, and bend
Your force to break, blow, burn, and make me new.
I, like an usurped town, to another due,
Labour to admit you, but Oh, to no end.
Reason, your viceroy in me, me should defend,
But is captived, and proves weak or untrue.
Yet dearly I love you, and would be loved fain,
But am betrothed unto your enemy:
Divorce me, untie or break that knot again,
Take me to you, imprison me, for I,
Except you enthrall me, never shall be free,
Nor ever chaste, except you ravish me.

A Hymn to God the Father

Wilt Thou forgive that sin where I begun,
    Which was my sin, though it were done before?
Wilt Thou forgive that sin through which I run,
    And do run still, though still I do deplore?
When Thou hast done, Thou hast not done;
      For I have more.
Wilt Thou forgive that sin which I have won
    Others to sin, and made my sins their door?
Wilt Thou forgive that sin which I did shun
    A year or two, but wallow'd in a score?
When Thou hast done, Thou hast not done;
      For I have more.
I have a sin of fear, that when I've spun
    My last thread, I shall perish on the shore;
But swear by Thyself that at my death Thy Son
    Shall shine as He shines now and heretofore:
And having done that, Thou hast done;
      I have no more.

John Milton

"The end of learning is to know God, and out of that knowledge to love Him and imitate Him"

When He Fled from Absalom

LORD how many are my foes
How many those
That in arms against me rise
Many are they
That of my life distrustfully thus say,
No help for him in God there lies.
But thou Lord art my shield my glory,
Thee through my story
Th' exalter of my head I count
Aloud I cry'd 10
Unto Jehovah, he full soon reply'd
And heard me from his holy mount.
I lay and slept, I wak'd again,
For my sustain
Was the Lord. Of many millions
The populous rout
I fear not though incamping round about
They pitch against me their Pavillions.
Rise Lord, save me my God for thou
Hast smote ere now 20
On the cheek-bone all my foes,
Of men abhor'd
Hast broke the teeth. This help was from the Lord;
Thy blessing on thy people flows.

Upon the Circumcision

Ye flaming Powers, and winged Warriours bright,
That erst with Musick, and triumphant song
First heard by happy watchful Shepherds ear,
So sweetly sung your Joy the Clouds along
Through the soft silence of the list'ning night;
Now mourn, and if sad share with us to bear
Your fiery essence can distill no tear,
Burn in your sighs, and borrow
Seas wept from our deep sorrow,
He who with all Heav'ns heraldry while are
Enter'd the world, now bleeds to give us ease;
Alas, how soon our sin
Sore doth begin
His Infancy to sease!
O more exceeding love or law more just?
Just law indeed, but more exceeding love !
For we by rightfull doom remediles
Were lost in death, till he that dwelt above
High thron'd in secret bliss, for us frail dust
Emptied his glory, ev'n to nakednes;
And that great Cov'nant which we still transgress
Intirely satisfi'd,
And the full wrath beside
Of vengeful Justice bore for our excess,
And seals obedience first with wounding smart
This day, but O ere long
Huge pangs and strong
Will pierce more neer his heart.

St. Frances

"I have been all things unholy. If God can work through me, he can work through anyone."

All Creatures of Our God and King

All creatures of our God and King
Lift up your voice and with us sing,
Alleluia! Alleluia!
Thou burning sun with golden beam,
Thou silver moon with softer gleam!
Thou rushing wind that art so strong
Ye clouds that sail in Heaven along,
O praise Him! Alleluia!
Thou rising moon, in praise rejoice,
Ye lights of evening, find a voice!
Thou flowing water, pure and clear,
Make music for thy Lord to hear,
O praise Him! Alleluia!
Thou fire so masterful and bright,
That givest man both warmth and light.
Dear mother earth, who day by day
Unfoldest blessings on our way,
O praise Him! Alleluia!
The flowers and fruits that in thee grow,
Let them His glory also show.
And all ye men of tender heart,
Forgiving others, take your part,
O sing ye! Alleluia!
Ye who long pain and sorrow bear,
Praise God and on Him cast your care
And thou most kind and gentle Death,
Waiting to hush our latest breath,
O praise Him! Alleluia!
Thou leadest home the child of God,
And Christ our Lord the way hath trod.
Let all things their Creator bless,
And worship Him in humbleness,
O praise Him! Alleluia!

Praise, praise the Father, praise the Son,
And praise the Spirit, Three in One!
O praise Him! O praise Him!
Alleluia! Alleluia! Alleluia!

John Bunyan

"Pray often; for prayer is a shield to the soul, a sacrifice to God, and a scourge for Satan"

A Boy and Watchmaker

This watch my father did on me bestow,
A golden one it is, but 'twill not go,
Unless it be at an uncertainty:
But as good none as one to tell a lie.
When 'tis high day my hand will stand at nine;
I think there's no man's watch so bad as mine.
Sometimes 'tis sullen, 'twill not go at all,
And yet 'twas never broke nor had a fall.

Watchmaker.

Your watch, though it be good, through want of skill
May fail to do according to your will.
Suppose the balance, wheels, and springs be good,
And all things else, unless you understood
To manage it, as watches ought to be,
Your watch will still be at uncertainty.
Come, tell me, do you keep it from the dust,
Yea, wind it also duly up you must?
Take heed, too, that you do not strain the spring;
You must be circumspect in every thing,
Or else your watch, were it as good again,

Would not with time and tide you entertain.

Comparison.

This boy an emblem is of a convert,
His watch of the work of grace within his heart,
The watchmaker is Jesus Christ our Lord,
His counsel, the directions of his Word;
Then convert, if thy heart be out of frame,
Of this watchmaker learn to mend the same.
Do not lay ope' thy heart to worldly dust,
Nor let thy graces over-grow with rust,
Be oft' renewed in the' spirit of thy mind,
Or else uncertain thou thy watch wilt find.

St. Methodius

"You Yourself, O Christ are my all. For you I keep myself chaste, and holding aloft my shining lamp I run to meet You, my Spouse,"

The Virgin's Song

The Bridegroom cometh! overhead
The shout descending wakes the dead!
Go forth to meet the King,
The gates just entering!
Virgins, white-robed, with lamps haste eastward forth to meet Him,
Haste ye, O haste to greet Him!

With holy feet, and lamps bright burning,
I go to meet my Lord returning.

Earth's mournful bliss I left, and toys
Of wanton life, and foolish joys:
To Thee alone I cling:
Thou art my Life, my King:
Grant that I may, O Blessèd, ever close to Thee,
Thy royal beauty see!

With holy feet, and lamps bright burning,
I go to meet my Lord returning.

Thou art my wealth: for Thee I fled
All worldly lure; and upward sped;
And come in spotless dress
Of Thine own Righteousness,
With Thee to enter in the bridal chamber gates,
Where perfect bliss awaits.

With holy feet, and lamps bright burning,
I go to meet my Lord returning.

Saved from the dragon's myriad wiles,
By which the simple he beguiles,
I bore the dreadful fire,

And wild beasts' savage ire;
Waiting till Thou from Heaven, O Hope of all creation,
shouldst come to my salvation!

With holy feet, and lamps bright burning,
I go to meet my Lord returning.

My home and country for Thy sake,
And maiden dance, I did forsake,
And mother's pride and race,
And thoughts of rank and place;
For Thou, O Christ the Word, art all in all to me:
I long for naught save Thee!

With holy feet, and lamps bright burning,
I go to meet my Lord returning.

Hail! Christ the Life, unchanging Day,
Accept this humble virgin lay:
To Thee our song of praise
With heart and voice we raise!
In Thee, O Thou perfection's flower, O Word Divine,
Love, joy, mind, wisdom, shine.
With holy feet, and lamps bright burning,
I go to meet my Lord returning.

O Bride, triumphant now in light,
And clad in robes of purest white,
Sweet-breathing, sinless, free,
Ope wide the gates to me:
Sit we in self-same company near Christ above,
And sing thy marriage, Love!

With holy feet, and lamps bright burning,
I go to meet my Lord returning.

Ah me! some virgins vainly pour
Their sobs and cries outside the door:
Their lamps are quenched, and they
No burning light display:
Their error they would mend: but ah! they come too late,
And closèd is the gate.

With holy feet, and lamps bright burning,
I go to meet my Lord returning.

For they a foolish part had played,
And from the sacred pathway strayed;
Oil, they had purchased none:
Ah! wretched and undone!
Forbidden with dead lamps the home of bliss to see,
They wail their misery.

With holy feet, and lamps bright burning,
I go to meet my Lord returning.

Lo! goblet filled with sweetest wine:
Drink we, O virgins, 'tis Divine;
And forth-set for our need:
Lo! this is drink indeed;
This for the guests, who to the marriage bidden are,
The Bridegroom doth prepare.

With holy feet, and lamps bright burning,
I go to meet my Lord returning.

First type, O Blessèd One, of Thee
In Abel shining bright we see:
To heaven he lifts his eyes,
Blood-dripping, and thus cries:
"Me, by my cruel brother slain, receive, O Lord,
O Thou the Eternal Word."

With holy feet, and lamps bright burning,
I go to meet my Lord returning.

Joseph, another type of Thee,
Won highest prize of purity:
Whom Thou wouldst own Thy child:
He scorned to be beguiled
By, shameless woman; stripped, he yet her wrath defied,
And straight to Thee he cried:

With holy feet, and lamps bright burning,
I go to meet my Lord returning.

A lamb for sacrifice is sought:
A lamb-like victim Jephthah brought:
For rash-made vow he cared,
Nor virgin daughter spared:
A type, O Blessèd One, of Thy humanity,
She poured her soul to Thee:

With holy feet, and lamps bright burning,
I go to meet my Lord returning.

In valour Judith holds high post:
The leader of the oppressing host
She smote by beauty's lure,
Herself a type all pure:
He headless lay; and unto Thee the conquering maid
Her love in song displayed:

With holy feet, and lamps bright burning,
I go to meet my Lord returning.

The Judges twain, by passion's flame

Enkindled, and all dead to shame,
Would chaste Susannah bind
To their unhallowed mind:
To their proposals base she gave a just reply:
And raised her voice on high:

With holy feet, and lamps bright burning,
I go to meet my Lord returning.

'Twere better far that I should die,
Than traitress be to marriage tie,
And yielding to your will
Both soul and body kill:
Base men! God's fire of wrath eternal would me seize:
Save me, O Christ, from these!

With holy feet, and lamps bright burning,
I go to meet my Lord returning.

And he who thousands washed from sin,
Of Thy true light the bringer-in,
For virtue's cause alone
Is into prison thrown
By wicked king: and staining now the ground with gore,
He cried to Thee the more:

With holy feet, and lamps bright burning,
I go to meet my Lord returning.

And Thy blest Mother, spotless maid,
Was thought her vows to have betrayed,
When travailing with Thee,
O Lord of purity:
And found with child of transcendental heavenly birth,
She raised her voice from earth:

With holy feet, and lamps bright burning,
I go to meet my Lord returning.
Thy saints, all eager that they may
Behold the glories of the day
Of Thine espousals high,
With holy gifts draw nigh:
For Thou, O Word, hast called them, Thou the angels'
King:
White-robed to Thee they sing.

With holy feet, and lamps bright burning,
I go to meet my Lord returning.

O holy Church, O heavenly Bride,
With hymns, attending at Thy side,
We yet on earth below
Thine honour thus forth-show:
All snow-white thou, all beauteous spouse of Christ above,
All purity, all love.
Songs and Hymns of the Earliest Greek Christian Poets

With holy feet, and lamps bright burning,
I go to meet my Lord returning.

Past are corruption, sickness, pain;
Nor tears shall ever flow again;
For troubles all have fled;
And death himself is dead:
And sin and folly with dark dismal train are gone,
Since grace in glory shone.

With holy feet, and lamps bright burning,
I go to meet my Lord returning.

No longer Paradise of men
Is void; for there God wills again

That man should safely dwell;
Yea, man the same who fell
Beneath the serpent's wiles: now in the promised rest,
Immortal, fearless, blest.

With holy feet, and lamps bright burning,
I go to meet my Lord returning.

Thou now to heavenly places raised,
By all the virgin choir art praised,
O Bride of Heavenly King:
And song all new we sing:
With lighted torch in hand, with snow-white lilies crowned,
Thy praise in Christ we sound.

With holy feet, and lamps bright burning,
I go to meet my Lord returning.

Father of heaven, supreme in might,
Dwelling in pure eternal light
With Thine own Son most dear,
Admit--for we are here--
E'en us within the gates of life, to sing Thy love
In Thy blest courts above.

With holy feet, and lamps bright burning,
I go to meet my Lord returning.

Clement of Alexandria

"The Lord has turned all our sunsets into sunrise."

Hymn to Christ

O Thou, the King of saints, all-conquering Word,
Son of the Highest, wisdom's Fount and Lord,
The prop that doth uphold through toil and pain;
The joy of ages through immortal reign;
Yet born of mortal flesh for life's brief span,
O Saviour Jesus, Shepherd, Husbandman;
Helm Thou to guide, and bridle to restrain,
Wing of the holy flock that heaven would gain;
Catcher of men from evil's whelming sea,
10 The holy fishes, saved that are to be,
Drawn from the billowy deep with sweetest lure
Of life that shall for evermore endure:
O holiest Shepherd of enlightened sheep,
Lead Thou Thy flock the upward heavenly steep:
O King of holy children, lead the way,
And pure may they both follow and obey!
Thou art, O Christ, the living heavenly Way,
The ever-flowing Word, unchanging Day,
Eternal Light, and mercy's healthful Spring;
The Perfecter of every virtuous thing;
Pure Life of all the happy ransomed throng
Who hymn their God through all the ages long:
The heavenly34 milk, from holy breasts that flows,
By which the infant Church in wisdom grows,
And graces rare, as it befits the Bride,
Adorned, O Jesu Christ, for Thine own side.
Thy feeble children gather with sweet smile,
To sing with holy mouth, and free from guile,
Thyself, in songs and praises without end,
30 The children's leader, and the children's friend.
O little children, thus so gently led,
So tenderly with truth and reason fed,
And filled with the Holy Spirit's dew,

Our hymns and praises feeble, yet all true,
In grateful homage unto Christ the King,
Who taught us life, let us together sing:
A peaceful choir, Christ-born, and undefiled,
A people wise, sing we the strong-born child;
Sing we with heart and voice, and never cease
To praise with one accord the God of Peace!

T.S. Eliot

"As things are, and as fundamentally they must always be, poetry is not a career, but a mug's game. No honest poet can ever feel quite sure of the permanent value of what he has written: He may have wasted his time and messed up his life for nothing."

The Hippopotamus

The broad-backed hippopotamus
Rests on his belly in the mud;
Although he seems so firm to us
He is merely flesh and blood.

Flesh-and-blood is weak and frail,
Susceptible to nervous shock;
While the True <u>Church</u> can never fail
For it is based upon a rock.

The hippo's feeble steps may err
In compassing material ends,
While the True Church need never stir
To gather in its dividends.

The 'potamus can never reach
The mango on the mango-tree;
But fruits of pomegranate and peach
Refresh the Church from over sea.

At mating time the hippo's voice
Betrays inflexions hoarse and odd,
But every week we hear rejoice
The Church, at being one with <u>God</u>.

The hippopotamus's day
Is passed in <u>sleep</u>; at <u>night</u> he hunts;
God works in a mysterious way-
The Church can sleep and feed at once.

I saw the 'potamus take wing
Ascending from the damp savannas,

And quiring <u>angels</u> round him sing
The praise of God, in loud hosannas.

Blood of the Lamb shall wash him clean
And him shall heavenly arms enfold,
Among the saints he shall be seen
Performing on a harp of gold.

He shall be washed as white as <u>snow</u>,
By all the martyr'd virgins kiss,
While the True Church remains below
Wrapt in the old miasmal mist.

Little Gidding
(No. 4 of 'Four Quartets')

I

Midwinter spring is its own season
Sempiternal though sodden towards sundown,
Suspended in time, between pole and tropic.
When the short day is brightest, with frost and fire,
The brief sun flames the ice, on pond and ditches,
In windless cold that is the heart's heat,
Reflecting in a watery mirror
A glare that is blindness in the early afternoon.
And glow more intense than blaze of branch, or brazier,
Stirs the dumb spirit: no wind, but pentecostal fire
In the dark time of the year. Between melting and freezing
The soul's sap quivers. There is no earth smell
Or smell of living thing. This is the spring time
But not in time's covenant. Now the hedgerow
Is blanched for an hour with transitory blossom
Of snow, a bloom more sudden
Than that of summer, neither budding nor fading,
Not in the scheme of generation.
Where is the summer, the unimaginable
Zero summer?
        If you came this way,
Taking the route you would be likely to take
From the place you would be likely to come from,
If you came this way in may time, you would find the hedges
White again, in May, with voluptuary sweetness.
It would be the same at the end of the journey,
If you came at night like a broken king,
If you came by day not knowing what you came for,
It would be the same, when you leave the rough road
And turn behind the pig-sty to the dull facade
And the tombstone. And what you thought you came for

Is only a shell, a husk of meaning
From which the purpose breaks only when it is fulfilled
If at all. Either you had no purpose
Or the purpose is beyond the end you figured
And is altered in fulfilment. There are other places
Which also are the world's end, some at the sea jaws,
Or over a dark lake, in a desert or a city—
But this is the nearest, in place and time,
Now and in England.
       If you came this way,
Taking any route, starting from anywhere,
At any time or at any season,
It would always be the same: you would have to put off
Sense and notion. You are not here to verify,
Instruct yourself, or inform curiosity
Or carry report. You are here to kneel
Where prayer has been valid. And prayer is more
Than an order of words, the conscious occupation
Of the praying mind, or the sound of the voice praying.
And what the dead had no speech for, when living,
They can tell you, being dead: the communication
Of the dead is tongued with fire beyond the language of the living.
Here, the intersection of the timeless moment
Is England and nowhere. Never and always.

II
Ash on and old man's sleeve
Is all the ash the burnt roses leave.
Dust in the air suspended
Marks the place where a story ended.
Dust inbreathed was a house—
The walls, the wainscot and the mouse,
The death of hope and despair,
    This is the death of air.

There are flood and drouth
Over the eyes and in the mouth,
Dead water and dead sand
Contending for the upper hand.
The parched eviscerate soil
Gapes at the vanity of toil,
Laughs without mirth.
    This is the death of earth.
Water and fire succeed
The town, the pasture and the weed.
Water and fire deride
The sacrifice that we denied.
Water and fire shall rot
The marred foundations we forgot,
Of sanctuary and choir.
    This is the death of water and fire.
In the uncertain hour before the morning
    Near the ending of interminable night
    At the recurrent end of the unending
After the dark dove with the flickering tongue
    Had passed below the horizon of his homing
    While the dead leaves still rattled on like tin
Over the asphalt where no other sound was
    Between three districts whence the smoke arose
    I met one walking, loitering and hurried
As if blown towards me like the metal leaves
    Before the urban dawn wind unresisting.
    And as I fixed upon the down-turned face
That pointed scrutiny with which we challenge
    The first-met stranger in the waning dusk
    I caught the sudden look of some dead master
Whom I had known, forgotten, half recalled
    Both one and many; in the brown baked features
    The eyes of a familiar compound ghost
Both intimate and unidentifiable.
    So I assumed a double part, and cried

    And heard another's voice cry: 'What! are you here?'
Although we were not. I was still the same,
    Knowing myself yet being someone other—
    And he a face still forming; yet the words sufficed
To compel the recognition they preceded.
    And so, compliant to the common wind,
    Too strange to each other for misunderstanding,
In concord at this intersection time
    Of meeting nowhere, no before and after,
    We trod the pavement in a dead patrol.
I said: 'The wonder that I feel is easy,
    Yet ease is cause of wonder. Therefore speak:
    I may not comprehend, may not remember.'
And he: 'I am not eager to rehearse
    My thoughts and theory which you have forgotten.
    These things have served their purpose: let them be.
So with your own, and pray they be forgiven
    By others, as I pray you to forgive
    Both bad and good. Last season's fruit is eaten
And the fullfed beast shall kick the empty pail.
    For last year's words belong to last year's language
    And next year's words await another voice.
But, as the passage now presents no hindrance
    To the spirit unappeased and peregrine
    Between two worlds become much like each other,
So I find words I never thought to speak
    In streets I never thought I should revisit
    When I left my body on a distant shore.
Since our concern was speech, and speech impelled us
    To purify the dialect of the tribe
    And urge the mind to aftersight and foresight,
Let me disclose the gifts reserved for age
    To set a crown upon your lifetime's effort.
    First, the cold friction of expiring sense
Without enchantment, offering no promise
    But bitter tastelessness of shadow fruit

As body and soul begin to fall asunder.
Second, the conscious impotence of rage
   At human folly, and the laceration
   Of laughter at what ceases to amuse.
And last, the rending pain of re-enactment
   Of all that you have done, and been; the shame
   Of motives late revealed, and the awareness
Of things ill done and done to others' harm
   Which once you took for exercise of virtue.
   Then fools' approval stings, and honour stains.
From wrong to wrong the exasperated spirit
   Proceeds, unless restored by that refining fire
   Where you must move in measure, like a dancer.'
The day was breaking. In the disfigured street
   He left me, with a kind of valediction,
   And faded on the blowing of the horn.

III

There are three conditions which often look alike
Yet differ completely, flourish in the same hedgerow:
Attachment to self and to things and to persons, detachment
From self and from things and from persons; and, growing between them, indifference
Which resembles the others as death resembles life,
Being between two lives—unflowering, between
The live and the dead nettle. This is the use of memory:
For liberation—not less of love but expanding
Of love beyond desire, and so liberation
From the future as well as the past. Thus, love of a country
Begins as attachment to our own field of action
And comes to find that action of little importance
Though never indifferent. History may be servitude,
History may be freedom. See, now they vanish,
The faces and places, with the self which, as it could, loved them,
To become renewed, transfigured, in another pattern.

Sin is Behovely, but
All shall be well, and
All manner of thing shall be well.
If I think, again, of this place,
And of people, not wholly commendable,
Of no immediate kin or kindness,
But of some peculiar genius,
All touched by a common genius,
United in the strife which divided them;
If I think of a king at nightfall,
Of three men, and more, on the scaffold
And a few who died forgotten
In other places, here and abroad,
And of one who died blind and quiet
Why should we celebrate
These dead men more than the dying?
It is not to ring the bell backward
Nor is it an incantation
To summon the spectre of a Rose.
We cannot revive old factions
We cannot restore old policies
Or follow an antique drum.
These men, and those who opposed them
And those whom they opposed
Accept the constitution of silence
And are folded in a single party.
Whatever we inherit from the fortunate
We have taken from the defeated
What they had to leave us—a symbol:
A symbol perfected in death.
And all shall be well and
All manner of thing shall be well
By the purification of the motive
In the ground of our beseeching.

IV

The dove descending breaks the air
With flame of incandescent terror
Of which the tongues declare
The one discharge from sin and error.
The only hope, or else despair
    Lies in the choice of pyre of pyre—
    To be redeemed from fire by fire.
Who then devised the torment? Love.
Love is the unfamiliar Name
Behind the hands that wove
The intolerable shirt of flame
Which human power cannot remove.
    We only live, only suspire
    Consumed by either fire or fire.

V

What we call the beginning is often the end
And to make and end is to make a beginning.
The end is where we start from. And every phrase
And sentence that is right (where every word is at home,
Taking its place to support the others,
The word neither diffident nor ostentatious,
An easy commerce of the old and the new,
The common word exact without vulgarity,
The formal word precise but not pedantic,
The complete consort dancing together)
Every phrase and every sentence is an end and a beginning,
Every poem an epitaph. And any action
Is a step to the block, to the fire, down the sea's throat
Or to an illegible stone: and that is where we start.
We die with the dying:
See, they depart, and we go with them.
We are born with the dead:
See, they return, and bring us with them.
The moment of the rose and the moment of the yew-tree
Are of equal duration. A people without history

Is not redeemed from time, for history is a pattern
Of timeless moments. So, while the light fails
On a winter's afternoon, in a secluded chapel
History is now and England.
With the drawing of this Love and the voice of this
    Calling

We shall not cease from exploration
And the end of all our exploring
Will be to arrive where we started
And know the place for the first time.
Through the unknown, unremembered gate
When the last of earth left to discover
Is that which was the beginning;
At the source of the longest river
The voice of the hidden waterfall
And the children in the apple-tree
Not known, because not looked for
But heard, half-heard, in the stillness
Between two waves of the sea.
Quick now, here, now, always—
A condition of complete simplicity
(Costing not less than everything)
And all shall be well and
All manner of thing shall be well
When the tongues of flame are in-folded
Into the crowned knot of fire
And the fire and the rose are one.

Journey of The Magi

'A cold coming we had of it,
Just the worst time of the year
For a journey, and such a long journey:
The ways deep and the weather sharp,
The very dead of winter.'
And the camels galled, sore-footed, refractory,
Lying down in the melting snow.
There were times we regretted
The summer palaces on slopes, the terraces,
And the silken girls bringing sherbet.
Then the camel men cursing and grumbling
And running away, and wanting their liquor and women,
And the night-fires going out, and the lack of shelters,
And the cities hostile and the towns unfriendly
And the villages dirty and charging high prices:
A hard time we had of it.
At the end we preferred to travel all night,
Sleeping in snatches,
With the voices singing in our ears, saying
That this was all folly.
Then at dawn we came down to a temperate valley,
Wet, below the snow line, smelling of vegetation;
With a running stream and a water-mill beating the darkness,
And three trees on the low sky,
And an old white horse galloped away in the meadow.
Then we came to a tavern with vine-leaves over the lintel,
Six hands at an open door dicing for pieces of silver,
And feet kicking the empty wine-skins.
But there was no information, and so we continued
And arrived at evening, not a moment too soon
Finding the place; it was (you may say) satisfactory.
All this was a long time ago, I remember,
And I would do it again, but set down

This set down
This: were we led all that way for
Birth or Death? There was a Birth, certainly,
We had evidence and no doubt. I had seen birth and death,
But had thought they were different; this Birth was
Hard and bitter agony for us, like Death, our death.
We returned to our places, these Kingdoms,
But no longer at ease here, in the <u>old dispensation</u>,
With an alien people clutching their gods.
I should be glad of another death.

The Wasteland

I. The Burial of the Dead
APRIL is the cruelest month, breeding
Lilacs out of the dead land, mixing
Memory and desire, stirring
Dull roots with spring rain.
Winter kept us warm, covering
Earth in forgetful snow, feeding
A little life with dried tubers.
Summer surprised us, coming over the
Starnbergersee*   [A lake near Munich]
With a shower of rain; we stopped in the colonnade
And went on in sunlight, into the
Hofgarten*,   [A park in Munich]
And drank coffee, and talked for an hour.
Bin gar keine Russin, stamm' aus Litauen, echt
deutsch.*   ['I am not Russian at all, I am
And when we were children, staying at the arch-
duke's,   a German from Lithuania']
My cousin's, he took me out on a sled,
And I was frightened. He said, Marie,
Marie, hold on tight. And down we went.
In the mountains, there you feel free.
I read, much of the night, and go south in winter.
What are the roots that clutch, what branches grow
Out of this stony rubbish? Son of man,
You cannot say, or guess, for you know only
A heap of broken images, where the sun beats,
And the dead tree gives no shelter, the cricket no relief,
And the dry stone no sound of water. Only
There is shadow under this red rock
(Come in under the shadow of this red rock),
And I will show you something different from either
Your shadow at morning striding behind you
Or your shadow at evening rising to meet you;

I will show you fear in a handful of dust.
Frisch weht der Wind* ['fresh blows the wind to the homeland']
Der heimat zu
Mein Irisch kind,* ['my Irish child, where do you linger?']
Wo weilest du?
"You gave me hyacinths first a year ago;"
"They called me the hyacinth girl."
--Yet when we came back, late, from the hyacinth garden,
Your arms full, and your hair wet, I could not
Speak, and my eyes failed, I was neither
Living nor dead, and I knew nothing,
Looking into the heart of light, the silence.
Oed' und leer das Meer. ['waste and empty is the sea']
Madame Sosostris, famous clairvoyante,
Has a bad cold, nevertheless
Is known to be the wisest woman in Europe,
With a wicked pack of cards. Here, said she,
Is your card, the drowned Phoenician Sailor.
(Those are pearls that were his eyes. Look!)
Here is Belladonna, the Lady of the Rocks,
The lady of situations.
Here is the man with three staves, and here the Wheel,
And here is the one-eyed merchant, and this card,
Which is blank, is something that he carries on his back,
Which I am forbidden to see. I do not find
The Hanged Man. Fear death by water.
I see crowds of people, walking round in a ring.
Thank you. If you see dear Mrs. Equitone,
Tell her I bring the horoscope myself;
One must be so careful these days.
Unreal City
Under the brown fog of a winter dawn,
A crowd flowed over London Bridge, so many,

I had not thought death had undone so many.
Sighs, short and infrequent, were exhaled,
And each man fixed his eyes before his feet,
Flowed up the hill and down King William Street
To where Saint Mary Woolnoth kept the hours
With a dead sound on the final stroke of nine.
There I saw one I knew, and stopped him, crying, "Stetson!
You who were with me in the ships at Mylae!
That corpse you planted last year in your garden,
Has it begun to sprout? Will it bloom this year?
Or has the sudden frost disturbed its bed?
Oh keep the Dog far hence, that's friend to men,
Or with his nails he'll dig it up again!
You! hypocrite lecteur!--mon semblable!--mon frère!"

II. A Game of Chess
The Chair she sat in, like a burnished throne,
Glowed on the marble, where the glass
Held up by standards wrought with fruited vines
From which a golden Cupidon peeped out
(Another hid his eyes behind his wing)
Doubled the flames of sevenbranched candelabra
Reflecting light upon the table as
The glitter of her jewels rose to meet it,
From satin cases poured in rich profusion.
In vials of ivory and colored glass,
Unstoppered, lurked her strange synthetic perfumes,
Unguent, powdered, or liquid--troubled, confused
And drowned the sense in odors; stirred by the air
That freshened from the window, these ascended
In fattening the prolonged candle-flames,
Stirring the pattern on the coffered ceiling.
Huge sea-wood fed with copper
Burned green and orange, framed by the coloured stone,
In which sad light a carved dolphin swam.
Above the antique mantle was displayed

As though a window gave upon the sylvan scene
The change of Philomel, by the barbarous king
So rudely forced; yet there the nightingale
Filled all the desert with inviolable voice
And still she cried, and still the world pursues,
"Jug Jug" to dirty ears.
And other withered stumps of time
Were told upon the walls; staring forms
Leaned out, leaning, hushing the world enclosed.
Footsteps shuffled on the stair.
Under the firelight, under the brush, her hair
Spread out in fiery points
Glowed into words, then would be savagely still.
"My nerves are bad tonight. Yes, bad. Stay with me.
"Speak to me. Why do you never speak. Speak.
  "What are you thinking of? What thinking? What?
"I never know what you are thinking. Think."

I think we are in rats' alley
Where the dead men lost their bones.
"What is that noise?"
           The wind under the door.
"What is that noise now? What is the wind doing?"
           Nothing again nothing.
         "Do
"You know nothing? Do you see nothing? Do you remember
"Nothing?"

  I remember
Those are pearls that were his eyes.
"Are you alive, or not? Is there nothing in your head?"
           But
O O O O that Shakespeherian Rag--
It's so elegant
So intelligent
"What shall I do now? What shall I do?"
"I shall rush out as I am, and walk the street

"With my hair down, so. What shall we do tomorrow?
"What shall we ever do?"
                                    The hot water at ten.
And, if it rains, a closed car at four.
And we shall play a game of chess,
Pressing lidless eyes and waiting for a knock upon the door.
When Lil's husband got demobbed, I said--
I didn't mince my words, I said to her myself,
HURRY UP PLEASE IT'S TIME*   [British call-out at pub closing time]
Now Albert's coming back, make yourself a bit smart.
He'll want to know what you done with that money he gave you
To get yourself some teeth. He did, I was there.
You have them all out, Lil, and get a nice set,
He said, I swear, I can't bear to look at you.
And no more can't I, I said, and think of poor Albert.
He's been in the army four years, he wants a good time.
And if you don't give it him, there's others will, I said.
Oh is there, she said. Something o' that, I said.
Then I'll know who to thank, she said, and give me a straight look.
HURRY UP PLEASE IT'S TIME
If you don't like it you can get on with it, I said.
Others can pick and choose if you can't.
But if Albert makes off, it won't be for lack of telling.
You ought to be ashamed, I said, to look so antique.
(And her only thirty-one.)
I can't help it, she said, pulling a long face,
It's them pills I took, to bring it off, she said.
(She's had five already, and nearly died of young George.)
The chemist said it would be all right, but I've never been the same.
You are a proper fool, I said.
Well, if Albert won't leave you alone, there it is, I said.

What you get married for if you don't want children?
HURRY UP PLEASE IT'S TIME
Well, that Sunday Albert was home, they had a hot gammon,
And they asked me in to dinner, to get the beauty of it hot--
HURRY UP PLEASE IT'S TIME
HURRY UP PLEASE IT'S TIME
Goonight Bill. Goonight Lou. Goonight May. Goonight.
Ta ta. Goonight. Goonight.
Good night, ladies, good night, sweet ladies, good night, good night.

III. The Fire Sermon
The river's tent is broken; the last fingers of leaf
Clutch and sink into the wet bank. The wind
Crosses the brown land, unheard. The nymphs are departed.
Sweet Thames, run softly, till I end my song.
The river bears no empty bottles, sandwich papers,
Silk handkerchiefs, cardboard boxes, cigarette ends
Or other testimony of summer nights. The nymphs are departed.
And their friends, the loitering heirs of city directors;
Departed, have left no addresses.
By the waters of Leman I sat down and wept . . .
Sweet Thames, run softly till I end my song,
Sweet Thames, run softly, for I speak not loud or long.
But at my back in a cold blast I hear
The rattle of the bones, and chuckle spread from ear to ear.
A rat crept softly through the vegetation
Dragging its slimy belly on the bank
While I sat fishing in the dull canal
On a winter evening round behind the gashouse
Musing upon the king my brother's wreck
And on the king my father's death before him.
White bodies naked on the low damp ground
And bones cast in a little low dry garret,

Rattled by the rat's foot only, year to year.
But at my back from time to time I hear
The sound of horns and motors, which shall bring
Sweeney to Mrs. Porter in the spring.
O the moon shone bright on Mrs. Porter
And on her daughter
They wash their feet in soda water
Et O ces voix d'enfants, chantant dans la coupole!
                          ['And oh, the voices of the children singing in the dome!']
Twit twit twit
Jug jug jug jug jug jug
So rudely forc'd
Tereu
Unreal City
Under the brown fog of a winter noon
Mr. Eugenides, the Smyrna merchant
C.i.f. London: documents at sight,
Asked me in demotic* French   [vulgar, common]
To luncheon at the Cannon Street Hotel
Followed by a weekend at the Metropole.
At the violet hour, when the eyes and back
Turn upward from the desk, when the human engine waits
Like a taxi throbbing waiting,
I Tiresias, though blind, throbbing between two lives,
Old man with wrinkled female breasts, can see
At the violet hour, the evening hour that strives
Homeward, and brings the sailor home from sea,
The typist home at teatime, clears her breakfast, lights
Her stove, and lays out food in tins.
Out of the window perilously spread
Her drying combinations touched by the sun's last rays,
On the divan are piled (at night her bed)
Stockings, slippers, camisoles and stays.
I Tiresias, old man with wrinkled dugs

Perceived the scene, and foretold the rest--
I too awaited the expected guest.
He, the young man carbuncular, arrives,
A small house agent's clerk, with a bold stare,
One of the low on whom assurance sits
As a silk hat on a Bradford millionaire.
The time is now propitious, as he guesses;
The meal is ended, she is bored and tired.
Endeavors to engage her in caresses
Which still are unreproved, if undesired.
Flushed and decided, he assaults at once;
Exploring hands encounter no defense.;
His vanity requires no response,
And makes a welcome of indifference.
(And I Tiresias have foresuffered all
Enacted on this same divan or bed;
I who have sat by Thebes below the wall
And walked among the lowest of the dead.)
Bestows one final patronizing kiss,
And gropes his way, finding the stairs unlit . . .
She turns and looks a moment in the glass,
Hardly aware of her departed lover;
Her brain allows one half-formed thought to pass:
"Well now that's done, and I'm glad it's over."
When lovely woman stoops to folly and
Paces about her room again, alone,
She smoothes her hair with automatic hand,
And puts a record on the gramophone.
"The music crept by me upon the waters",
And along the Strand, up Queen Victoria Street.
O City city, I can sometimes hear
Beside a public bar in Lower Thames Street,
The pleasant whining of a mandoline
And a clatter and a chatter from within
Where fishmen lounge at noon: where the walls
Of Magnus Martyr hold

Inexplicable splendor of Ionian white and gold.
    The river sweats
    Oil and tar
    The barges drift
    With the turning tide
    Red sails
    Wide
    To leeward, swing on the heavy spar.
    The barges wash
    Drifting logs
    Down Greenwich reach
    Past the Isle of Dogs.
        Weialala leia
        Wallala leialala
    Elizabeth and Leicester
    Beating oars
    The stern was formed
    A gilded shell
    Red and gold
    The brisk swell
    Rippled both shores
    Southwest wind
    Carried down stream
    The peal of bells
    White towers
        Weialala leia
        Wallala leialala
"Trams and dusty trees.
Highbury bore me. Richmond and Kew
Undid me. By Richmond I raised my knees
Supine on the floor of a narrow canoe."
"My feet are at Moorgate, and my heart
Under my feet. After the event
He wept. He promised `a new start.'
I made no comment. What should I resent?"
"On Margate Sands

I can connect
Nothing with nothing.
The broken fingernails of dirty hands
My people humble people who expect
Nothing."
        la la
To Carthage then I came
Burning burning burning burning
O Lord thou pluckest me out
O Lord thou pluckest
burning

IV. A Death by Water
Phlebas the Phoenician, a fortnight dead,
Forgot the cry of gulls, the deep sea swell
And the profit and loss.
        A current under sea
Picked his bones in whispers. As he rose and fell
He passed the stages of his age and youth,
Entering the whirlpool.
        Gentile or Jew
O you who turn the wheel and look to windward,
Consider Phlebas, who was once handsome and tall as you.

V. What the Thunder Said
After the torchlight red on sweaty faces
After the frosty silence in the gardens
After the agony in stony places
The shouting and the crying
Prison and palace and reverberation
Of thunder of spring over distant mountains
He who was living is now dead
We who were living are now dying
With a little patience
Here is no water but only rock
Rock and no water and the sandy road

The road winding above among the mountains
Which are mountains of rock without water
If there were water we should stop and drink
Amongst the rock one cannot stop or think
Sweat is dry and feet are in the sand
If there were only water amongst the rock
Dead mountain mouth of carious teeth that cannot spit
Here one can neither stand nor lie nor sit
There is not even silence in the mountains
But dry sterile thunder without rain
There is not even solitude in the mountains
But red sullen faces sneer and snarl
From doors of mudcracked houses
                              If there were water
And no rock
If there were rock
And also water
And water
A spring
A pool among the rock
If there were the sound of water only
Not the cicada
And dry grass singing
But sound of water over a rock
Where the hermit-thrush sings in the pine trees
Drip drop drip drop drop drop drop
But here there is no water
Who is the third who walks always beside you?
When I count, there are only you and I together
But when I look ahead, up the white road
There is always another one walking beside you,
Gliding wrapt in a brown mantle, hooded
I do not know whether a man or a woman
--But who is that on the other side of you?
What is that sound high in the air
Murmur of maternal lamentation

Who are those hooded hordes swarming
Over endless plains, stumbling in cracked earth
Ringed by the flat horizon only
What is the city over the mountains
Cracks and reforms and bursts in violet air
Falling towers
Jerusalem Athens Alexandria
Vienna London
Unreal
A woman drew her long black hair out tight
And fiddled whisper music on those strings
And bats with baby faces in the violet light
Whistled, and beat their wings
And crawled head downward down a blackened wall
And upside down in air were towers
Tolling reminiscent bells, that kept the hours
And voices singing out of empty cisterns and exhausted wells.
In this decayed hole among the mountains,
In the faint moonlight, the grass is singing
Over the tumbled graves, about the chapel
There is the empty chapel, only the wind's home.
It has no windows, and the door swings,
Dry bones can harm no one.
Only a cock stood on the rooftree
Co co rico co co rico
In a flash of lightning. Then a damp gust
Bringing rain
Ganga was sunken, and the limp leaves
Waited for rain, while the black clouds
Gathered far distant, over Himavant.
The jungle crouched, humped in silence.
Then spoke the thunder
DA
Datta: what have we given?
My friend, blood shaking my heart

The awful daring of a moment's surrender
Which an age of prudence can never retract,
By this, and this only, we have existed,
Which is not to be found in our obituaries
Or in memories draped by the beneficent spider
Or under seals broken by the lean solicitor
In our empty rooms
DA
Dayadhvam: I have heard the key
Turn in the door once and turn once only
We think of the key, each in his prison
Thinking of the key, each confirms his prison
Only at nightfall, aethereal rumors
Revive for a moment a broken Coriolanus
DA
Damyata: the boat responded
Gaily, to the hand expert with sail and oar
The sea was calm, your heart would have responded
Gaily, when invited, beating obedient
To controlling hands
     I sat upon the shore
Fishing, with the arid plain behind me
Shall I at least set my lands in order?
London bridge is falling down falling down falling down
Poi s'ascose nel foco che gli affina
Quando fiam uti chelidon--O swallow swallow
Le prince d'Aquitaine a la tour abolie
These fragments I have shored against my ruins
Why then Ile fit you. Hieronymo's mad againe.
Da. Dayadhvam. Damyata. [from a Hindu fable: 'Give, have compassion, have self control']
    Shantih shantih shantih [from a Hindu mantra: 'Peace...peace...peace']

Robert Service

"Be sure your wisest words are those you do not say."

The Call of the Wild

Have you gazed on naked grandeur where there's nothing else to gaze on,
    Set pieces and drop-curtain scenes galore,
Big mountains heaved to heaven, which the blinding sunsets blazon,
    Black canyons where the rapids rip and roar?
Have you swept the visioned valley with the green stream streaking through it,
    Searched the Vastness for a something you have lost?
Have you strung your soul to silence? Then for God's sake go and do it;
    Hear the challenge, learn the lesson, pay the cost.
Have you wandered in the wilderness, the sagebrush desolation,
    The bunch-grass levels where the cattle graze?
Have you whistled bits of rag-time at the end of all creation,
    And learned to know the desert's little ways?
Have you camped upon the foothills, have you galloped o'er the ranges,
    Have you roamed the arid sun-lands through and through?
Have you chummed up with the mesa? Do you know its moods and changes?
    Then listen to the Wild — it's calling you.
Have you known the Great White Silence, not a snow-gemmed twig aquiver?
    (Eternal truths that shame our soothing lies).
Have you broken trail on snowshoes? mushed your huskies up the river,
    Dared the unknown, led the way, and clutched the prize?
Have you marked the map's void spaces, mingled with the mongrel races,

  Felt the savage strength of brute in every thew?
And though grim as hell the worst is, can you round it off with curses?
  Then hearken to the Wild — it's wanting you.
Have you suffered, starved and triumphed, groveled down, yet grasped at glory,
  Grown bigger in the bigness of the whole?
"Done things" just for the doing, letting babblers tell the story,
  Seeing through the nice veneer the naked soul?
Have you seen God in His splendors, heard the text that nature renders?
  (You'll never hear it in the family pew).
The simple things, the true things, the silent men who do things —
  Then listen to the Wild — it's calling you.
They have cradled you in custom, they have primed you with their preaching,
  They have soaked you in convention through and through;
They have put you in a showcase; you're a credit to their teaching —
  But can't you hear the Wild? — it's calling you.
Let us probe the silent places, let us seek what luck betide us;
  Let us journey to a lonely land I know.
There's a whisper on the night-wind, there's a star agleam to guide us,
  And the Wild is calling, calling. . .let us go.

Spell of the Yukon

I wanted the gold, and I sought it;
I scrabbled and mucked like a slave.
Was it famine or scurvy - I fought it,
I hurled my youth into the grave.
I wanted the gold and I got it -
Came out with a fortune last fall, -
Yet somehow life's not what I thought it,
And somehow the gold isn't all.

No! There's the land. (Have you seen it?)
It's the cussedest land that I know,
From the big, dizzy mountains that screen it,
To the deep, deathlike valleys below.
Some say God was tired when He made it;
Some say it's a fine land to shun;
Maybe: but there's some as would trade it
For no land on earth - and I'm one.

You come to get rich (damned good reason),
You feel like an exile at first;
You hate it like hell for a season,
And then you are worse than the worst.
It grips you like some kinds of sinning;
It twists you from foe to a friend;
It seems it's been since the beginning;
It seems it will be to the end.

I've stood in some mighty-mouthed hollow
That's plumb-full of hush to the brim;
I've watched the big, husky sun wallow
In crimson and gold, and grow dim,
Till the moon set the pearly peaks gleaming,
And the stars tumbled out, neck and crop;
And I've thought that I surely was dreaming,

With the peace o' the world piled on top.

The summer - no sweeter was ever;
The sunshiny woods all athrill;
The grayling aleap in the river,
The bighorn asleep on the hill.
The strong life that never knows harness;
The wilds where the caribou call;
The freshness, the freedom, the farness -
O God! how I'm stuck on it all.

The winter! the brightness that blinds you,
The white land locked tight as a drum,
The cold fear that follows and finds you,
The silence that bludgeons you dumb.
The snows that are older than history,
The woods where the weird shadows slant;
The stillness, the moonlight, the mystery,
I've bade 'em good-bye - but I can't.

There's a land where the mountains are   nameless,
And the rivers all run God knows where;
There are lives that are erring and aimless,
And deaths that just hang by a hair;
There are hardships that nobody reckons;
There are valleys unpeopled and still;
There's a land - oh, it beckons and beckons,
And I want to go back - and I will.

They're making my money diminish;
I'm sick of the taste of champagne.
Thank God! when I'm skinned to a finish
I'll pike to the Yukon again.
I'll fight - and you bet it's no sham-fight;
It's hell! - but I've been there before;
And it's better than this by a dam site -

So me for the Yukon once more.

There's gold, and it's haunting and haunting;
It's luring me on as of old;
Yet it isn't the gold that I'm wanting,
So much as just finding the gold.
It's the great, big, broad land 'way up yonder,
It's the forests where silence has lease;
It's the beauty that thrills me with wonder,
It's the stillness that fills me with peace.

The Woman and the Angel

An angel was tired of heaven, as he lounged in the golden street;
His halo was tilted sideways, and his harp lay mute at his feet;
So the Master stooped in His pity, and gave him a pass to go,
For the space of a moon, to the earth-world, to mix with the men below.

He doffed his celestial garments, scarce waiting to lay them straight;
He bade goodbye to Peter, who stood by the golden gate;
The sexless singers of heaven chanted a fond farewell,
And the imps looked up as they pattered on the red-hot flags of hell.

Never was seen such an angel: eyes of a heavenly blue,
Features that shamed Apollo, hair of a golden hue;
The women simply adored him, his lips were like Cupid's bow;
But he never ventured to use them - and so they voted him slow.

Till at last there came One Woman, a marvel of loveliness,
And she whispered to him: "Do you love me?" And he answered that woman, "Yes."
And she said: "Put your arms around me, and kiss me, and hold me - so - "
But fiercely he drew back, saying: "This thing is wrong, and I know."

Then sweetly she mocked his scruples, and softly she him beguiled:

"You, who are verily man among men, speak with the tongue of a child.

We have outlived the old standards; we have burst, like an over-tight thong,

The ancient, outworn, puritanic traditions of Right and Wrong."

Then the Master feared for His angel, and called him again to His side,

For oh, the woman was wondrous, and oh, the angel was tried.

And deep in his hell sang the Devil, and this was the strain of his song:

"The ancient, outworn, puritanic traditions of Right and Wrong."

Clive Hamilton
(C.S. Lewis)

"I believe in Christianity as I believe that the sun has risen: not only because I see it, but because by it I see everything else."

Spirits in Bondage
Prologue

As of old Phoenician men, to the Tin Isles sailing
Straight against the sunset and the edges of the earth,
Chaunted loud above the storm and the strange sea's wailing,
Legends of their people and the land that gave them birth-
Sang aloud to Baal-Peor, sang unto the horned maiden,
Sang how they should come again with the Brethon treasure laden,
Sang of all the pride and glory of their hardy enterprise,
How they found the outer islands, where the unknown stars arise;
And the rowers down below, rowing hard as they could row,
Toiling at the stroke and feather through the wet and weary weather,
Even they forgot their burden in the measure of a song,
And the merchants and the masters and the bondsmen all together,
Dreaming of the wondrous islands, brought the gallant ship along;
So in mighty deeps alone on the chainless breezes blown
In my coracle of verses I will sing of lands unknown,
Flying from the scarlet city where a Lord that knows no pity,
Mocks the broken people praying round his iron throne,
-Sing about the Hidden Country fresh and full of quiet green.
Sailing over seas uncharted to a port that none has seen.

Part I The Prison House

I. Satan Speaks

I am Nature, the Mighty Mother,
I am the law: ye have none other.

I am the flower and the dewdrop fresh,
I am the lust in your itching flesh.

I am the battle's filth and strain,
I am the widow's empty pain.

I am the sea to smother your breath,
I am the bomb, the falling death.

I am the fact and the crushing reason
To thwart your fantasy's new-born treason.

I am the spider making her net,
I am the beast with jaws blood-wet.

I am a wolf that follows the sun
And I will catch him ere day be done.

II. French Nocturne (Monchy-Le-Preux)

Long leagues on either hand the trenches spread
And all is still; now even this gross line
Drinks in the frosty silences divine
The pale, green moon is riding overhead.

The jaws of a sacked village, stark and grim;
Out on the ridge have swallowed up the sun,
And in one angry streak his blood has run
To left and right along the horizon dim.

There comes a buzzing plane: and now, it seems
Flies straight into the moon. Lo! where he steers

Across the pallid globe and surely nears
In that white land some harbour of dear dreams!

False mocking fancy! Once I too could dream,
Who now can only see with vulgar eye
That he's no nearer to the moon than I
And she's a stone that catches the sun's beam.

What call have I to dream of anything?
I am a wolf. Back to the world again,
And speech of fellow-brutes that once were men
Our throats can bark for slaughter: cannot sing.

III. The Satyr

When the flowery hands of spring
Forth their woodland riches fling,
Through the meadows, through the valleys
Goes the satyr carolling.

From the mountain and the moor,
Forest green and ocean shore
All the faerie kin he rallies
Making music evermore.

See! the shaggy pelt doth grow
On his twisted shanks below,
And his dreadful feet are cloven
Though his brow be white as snow-

Though his brow be clear and white
And beneath it fancies bright,
Wisdom and high thoughts are woven
And the musics of delight,

Though his temples too be fair

Yet two horns are growing there
Bursting forth to part asunder
All the riches of his hair.

Faerie maidens he may meet
Fly the horns and cloven feet,
But, his sad brown eyes with wonder
Seeing-stay from their retreat.

IV. Victory

Roland is dead, Cuchulain's crest is low,
The battered war-rear wastes and turns to rust,
And Helen's eyes and Iseult's lips are dust
And dust the shoulders and the breasts of snow.

The faerie people from our woods are gone,
No Dryads have I found in all our trees,
No Triton blows his horn about our seas
And Arthur sleeps far hence in Avalon.

The ancient songs they wither as the grass
And waste as doth a garment waxen old,
All poets have been fools who thought to mould
A monument more durable than brass.

For these decay: but not for that decays
The yearning, high, rebellious spirit of man
That never rested yet since life began
From striving with red Nature and her ways.

Now in the filth of war, the baresark shout
Of battle, it is vexed. And yet so oft
Out of the deeps, of old, it rose aloft
That they who watch the ages may not doubt.

Though often bruised, oft broken by the rod,
Yet, like the phoenix, from each fiery bed
Higher the stricken spirit lifts its head
And higher-till the beast become a god.

V. Irish Nocturne

Now the grey mist comes creeping up
From the waste ocean's weedy strand
And fills the valley, as a cup
If filled of evil drink in a wizard's hand;
And the trees fade out of sight,
Like dreary ghosts unhealthily,
Into the damp, pale night,
Till you almost think that a clearer eye could see
Some shape come up of a demon seeking apart
His meat, as Grendel sought in Harte
The thanes that sat by the wintry log-
Grendel or the shadowy mass
Of Balor, or the man with the face of clay,
The grey, grey walker who used to pass
Over the rock-arch nightly to his prey.
But here at the dumb, slow stream where the willows hang,
With never a wind to blow the mists apart,
Bitter and bitter it is for thee. O my heart,
Looking upon this land, where poets sang,
Thus with the dreary shroud
Unwholesome, over it spread,
And knowing the fog and the cloud
In her people's heart and head
Even as it lies for ever upon her coasts
Making them dim and dreamy lest her sons should ever arise
And remember all their boasts;
For I know that the colourless skies
And the blurred horizons breed

Lonely desire and many words and brooding and never a deed.

VI. Spooks

Last night I dreamed that I was come again
Unto the house where my beloved dwells
After long years of wandering and pain.

And I stood out beneath the drenching rain
And all the street was bare, and black with night,
But in my true love's house was warmth and light.

Yet I could not draw near nor enter in,
And long I wondered if some secret sin
Or old, unhappy anger held me fast;

Till suddenly it came into my head
That I was killed long since and lying dead—
Only a homeless wraith that way had passed.

So thus I found my true love's house again
And stood unseen amid the winter night
And the lamp burned within, a rosy light,
And the wet street was shining in the rain.

VII. Apology

If men should ask, Despoina, why I tell
Of nothing glad nor noble in my verse
To lighten hearts beneath this present curse
And build a heaven of dreams in real hell,

Go you to them and speak among them thus:
"There were no greater grief than to recall,
Down in the rotting grave where the lithe worms crawl,
Green fields above that smiled so sweet to us."

Is it good to tell old tales of Troynovant
Or praises of dead heroes, tried and sage,
Or sing the queens of unforgotten age,
Brynhild and Maeve and virgin Bradamant?

How should I sing of them? Can it be good
To think of glory now, when all is done,
And all our labour underneath the sun
Has brought us this-and not the thing we would?

All these were rosy visions of the night,
The loveliness and wisdom feigned of old.
But now we wake. The East is pale and cold,
No hope is in the dawn, and no delight.

VIII. Ode for New Year's Day

Woe unto you, ye sons of pain that are this day in earth,
Now cry for all your torment: now curse your hour of birth
And the fathers who begat you to a portion nothing worth.
And Thou, my own beloved, for as brave as ere thou art,
Bow down thine head, Despoina, clasp thy pale arms over it,
Lie low with fast-closed eyelids, clenched teeth, enduring heart,
For sorrow on sorrow is coming wherein all flesh has part.
The sky above is sickening, the clouds of God's hate cover it,
Body and soul shall suffer beyond all word or thought,
Till the pain and noisy terror that these first years have wrought
Seem but the soft arising and prelude of the storm
That fiercer still and heavier with sharper lightnings fraught
Shall pour red wrath upon us over a world deform.

Thrice happy, O Despoina, were the men who were alive
In the great age and the golden age when still the cycle ran
On upward curve and easily, for them both maid and man
And beast and tree and spirit in the green earth could thrive.
But now one age is ending, and God calls home the stars
And looses the wheel of the ages and sends it spinning back
Amid the death of nations, and points a downward track,
And madness is come over us and great and little wars.
He has not left one valley, one isle of fresh and green
Where old friends could forgather amid the howling wreck.
It's vainly we are praying. We cannot, cannot check
The Power who slays and puts aside the beauty that has been.

It's truth they tell, Despoina, none hears the heart's complaining
For Nature will not pity, nor the red God lend an ear,
Yet I too have been mad in the hour of bitter paining
And lifted up my voice to God, thinking that he could hear
The curse wherewith I cursed Him because the Good was dead.
But lo! I am grown wiser, knowing that our own hearts
Have made a phantom called the Good, while a few years have sped
Over a little planet. And what should the great Lord know of it
Who tosses the dust of chaos and gives the suns their parts?
Hither and thither he moves them; for an hour we see the show of it:
Only a little hour, and the life of the race is done.
And here he builds a nebula, and there he slays a sun
And works his own fierce pleasure. All things he shall fulfill,
And O, my poor Despoina, do you think he ever hears
The wail of hearts he has broken, the sound of human ill?
He cares not for our virtues, our little hopes and fears,

And how could it all go on, love, if he knew of laughter and tears?

Ah, sweet, if a man could cheat him! If you could flee away
Into some other country beyond the rosy West,
To hide in the deep forests and be for ever at rest
From the rankling hate of God and the outworn world's decay!

IX. Night

After the fret and failure of this day,
And weariness of thought, O Mother Night,
Come with soft kiss to soothe our care away
And all our little tumults set to right;
Most pitiful of all death's kindred fair,
Riding above us through the curtained air
On thy dusk car, thou scatterest to the earth
Sweet dreams and drowsy charms of tender might
And lovers' dear delight before to-morrow's birth.
Thus art thou wont thy quiet lands to leave
And pillared courts beyond the Milky Way,
Wherein thou tarriest all our solar day
While unsubstantial dreams before thee weave
A foamy dance, and fluttering fancies play
About thy palace in the silver ray
Of some far, moony globe. But when the hour,
The long-expected comes, the ivory gates
Open on noiseless hinge before thy bower
Unbidden, and the jewelled chariot waits
With magic steeds. Thou from the fronting rim
Bending to urge them, whilst thy sea-dark hair
Falls in ambrosial ripples o'er each limb,
With beautiful pale arms, untrammelled, bare
For horsemanship, to those twin chargers fleet
Dost give full rein across the fires that glow

In the wide floor of heaven, from off their feet
Scattering the powdery star-dust as they go.
Come swiftly down the sky, O Lady Night,
Fall through the shadow-country, O most kind,
Shake out thy strands of gentle dreams and light
For chains, wherewith thou still art used to bind
With tenderest love of careful leeches' art
The bruised and weary heart
In slumber blind.

X. To Sleep

I will find out a place for thee, O Sleep-
A hidden wood among the hill-tops green,
Full of soft streams and little winds that creep
The murmuring boughs between.

A hollow cup above the ocean placed
Where nothing rough, nor loud, nor harsh shall be,
But woodland light and shadow interlaced
And summer sky and sea.

There in the fragrant twilight I will raise
A secret altar of the rich sea sod,
Whereat to offer sacrifice and praise
Unto my lonely god:

Due sacrifice of his own drowsy flowers,
The deadening poppies in an ocean shell
Round which through all forgotten days and hours
The great seas wove their spell.

So may he send me dreams of dear delight
And draughts of cool oblivion, quenching pain,
And sweet, half-wakeful moments in the night
To hear the falling rain.

And when he meets me at the dusk of day
To call me home for ever, this I ask-
That he may lead me friendly on that way
And wear no frightful mask.

XI. In Prison

I cried out for the pain of man,
I cried out for my bitter wrath
Against the hopeless life that ran
For ever in a circling path
From death to death since all began;
Till on a summer night
I lost my way in the pale starlight
And saw our planet, far and small,
Through endless depths of nothing fall
A lonely pin-prick spark of light,
Upon the wide, enfolding night,
With leagues on leagues of stars above it,
And powdered dust of stars below-
Dead things that neither hate nor love it
Not even their own loveliness can know,
Being but cosmic dust and dead.
And if some tears be shed,
Some evil God have power,
Some crown of sorrow sit
Upon a little world for a little hour-
Who shall remember? Who shall care for it?

XII. De Profundis

Come let us curse our Master ere we die,
For all our hopes in endless ruin lie.
The good is dead. Let us curse God most High.

Four thousand years of toil and hope and thought
Wherein man laboured upward and still wrought
New worlds and better, Thou hast made as naught.

We built us joyful cities, strong and fair,
Knowledge we sought and gathered wisdom rare.
And all this time you laughed upon our care,

And suddenly the earth grew black with wrong,
Our hope was crushed and silenced was our song,
The heaven grew loud with weeping. Thou art strong.

Come then and curse the Lord. Over the earth
Gross darkness falls, and evil was our birth
And our few happy days of little worth.

Even if it be not all a dream in vain
-The ancient hope that still will rise again-
Of a just God that cares for earthly pain,

Yet far away beyond our labouring night,
He wanders in the depths of endless light,
Singing alone his musics of delight;

Only the far, spent echo of his song
Our dungeons and deep cells can smite along,
And Thou art nearer. Thou art very strong.
O universal strength, I know it well,
It is but froth of folly to rebel;
For thou art Lord and hast the keys of Hell.

Yet I will not bow down to thee nor love thee,
For looking in my own heart I can prove thee,
And know this frail, bruised being is above thee.

Our love, our hope, our thirsting for the right,

Our mercy and long seeking of the light,
Shall we change these for thy relentless might?

Laugh then and slay. Shatter all things of worth,
Heap torment still on torment for thy mirth-
Thou art not Lord while there are Men on earth.

XIII. Satan Speaks

I am the Lord your God: even he that made
Material things, and all these signs arrayed
Above you and have set beneath the race
Of mankind, who forget their Father's face
And even while they drink my light of day
Dream of some other gods and disobey
My warnings, and despise my holy laws,
Even tho' their sin shall slay them. For which cause,
Dreams dreamed in vain, a never-filled desire
And in close flesh a spiritual fire,
A thirst for good their kind shall not attain,
A backward cleaving to the beast again.
A loathing for the life that I have given,
A haunted, twisted soul for ever riven
Between their will and mine-such lot I give
White still in my despite the vermin live.
They hate my world! Then let that other God
Come from the outer spaces glory-shod,
And from this castle I have built on Night
Steal forth my own thought's children into light,
If such an one there be. But far away
He walks the airy fields of endless day,
And my rebellious sons have called Him long
And vainly called. My order still is strong
And like to me nor second none I know.
Whither the mammoth went this creature too shall go.

XIV. The Witch

Trapped amid the woods with guile
They've led her bound in fetters vile
To death, a deadlier sorceress
Than any born for earth's distress
Since first the winner of the fleece
Bore home the Colchian witch to Greece-
Seven months with snare and gin
They've sought the maid o'erwise within
The forest's labyrinthine shade.
The lonely woodman half afraid
Far off her ragged form has seen
Sauntering down the alleys green,
Or crouched in godless prayer alone
At eve before a Druid stone.
But now the bitter chase is won,
The quarry's caught, her magic's done,
The bishop's brought her strongest spell
To naught with candle, book, and bell;
With holy water splashed upon her,
She goes to burning and dishonour
Too deeply damned to feel her shame,
For, though beneath her hair of flame
Her thoughtful head be lowly bowed
It droops for meditation proud
Impenitent, and pondering yet
Things no memory can forget,
Starry wonders she has seen
Brooding in the wildwood green
With holiness. For who can say
In what strange crew she loved to play,
What demons or what gods of old
Deep mysteries unto her have told
At dead of night in worship bent
At ruined shrines magnificent,

Or how the quivering will she sent
Alone into the great alone
Where all is loved and all is known,
Who now lifts up her maiden eyes
And looks around with soft surprise
Upon the noisy, crowded square,
The city oafs that nod and stare,
The bishop's court that gathers there,
The faggots and the blackened stake
Where sinners die for justice' sake?
Now she is set upon the pile,
The mob grows still a little while,
Till lo! before the eager folk
Up curls a thin, blue line of smoke.
"Alas!" the full-fed burghers cry,
"That evil loveliness must die!"

XV. Dungeon Grates

So piteously the lonely soul of man
Shudders before this universal plan,
So grievous is the burden and the pain,
So heavy weighs the long, material chain
From cause to cause, too merciless for hate,
The nightmare march of unrelenting fate,
I think that he must die thereof unless
Ever and again across the dreariness
There came a sudden glimpse of spirit faces,
A fragrant breath to tell of flowery places
And wider oceans, breaking on the shore
From which the hearts of men are always sore.
It lies beyond endeavour; neither prayer
Nor fasting, nor much wisdom winneth there,
Seeing how many prophets and wise men
Have sought for it and still returned again
With hope undone. But only the strange power

Of unsought Beauty in some casual hour
Can build a bridge of light or sound or form
To lead you out of all this strife and storm;
When of some beauty we are grown a part
Till from its very glory's midmost heart
Out leaps a sudden beam of larger light
Into our souls. All things are seen aright
Amid the blinding pillar of its gold,
Seven times more true than what for truth we hold
In vulgar hours. The miracle is done
And for one little moment we are one
With the eternal stream of loveliness
That flows so calm, aloft from all distress
Yet leaps and lives around us as a fire
Making us faint with overstrong desire
To sport and swim for ever in its deep-
Only a moment.
O! but we shall keep
Our vision still. One moment was enough,
We know we are not made of mortal stuff.
And we can bear all trials that come after,
The hate of men and the fool's loud bestial laughter
And Nature's rule and cruelties unclean,
For we have seen the Glory-we have seen.

XVI. The Philosopher

Who shall be our prophet then,
Chosen from all the sons of men
To lead his fellows on the way
Of hidden knowledge, delving deep
To nameless mysteries that keep
Their secret from the solar day!
Or who shall pierce with surer eye!
This shifting veil of bittersweet
And find the real things that lie

Beyond this turmoil, which we greet
With such a wasted wealth of tears?
Who shall cross over for us the bridge of fears
And pass in to the country where the ancient Mothers dwell?
Is it an elder, bent and hoar
Who, where the waste Atlantic swell
On lonely beaches makes its roar,
In his solitary tower
Through the long night hour by hour
Pores on old books with watery eye
When all his youth has passed him by,
And folly is schooled and love is dead
And frozen fancy laid abed,
While in his veins the gradual blood
Slackens to a marish flood?
For he rejoiceth not in the ocean's might,
Neither the sun giveth delight,
Nor the moon by night
Shall call his feet to wander in the haunted forest lawn.
He shall no more rise suddenly in the dawn
When mists are white and the dew lies pearly
Cold and cold on every meadow,
To take his joy of the season early,
The opening flower and the westward shadow,
And scarcely can he dream of laughter and love,
They lie so many leaden years behind.
Such eyes are dim and blind,
And the sad, aching head that nods above
His monstrous books can never know
The secret we would find.
But let our seer be young and kind
And fresh and beautiful of show,
And taken ere the lustyhead
And rapture of his youth be dead;
Ere the gnawing, peasant reason

School him over-deep in treason
To the ancient high estate
Of his fancy's principate,
That he may live a perfect whole,
A mask of the eternal soul,
And cross at last the shadowy bar
To where the ever-living are.

XVII. The Ocean Strand

O leave the labouring roadways of the town,
The shifting faces and the changeful hue
Of markets, and broad echoing streets that drown
The heart's own silent music. Though they too
Sing in their proper rhythm, and still delight
The friendly ear that loves warm human kind,
Yet it is good to leave them all behind,
Now when from lily dawn to purple night
Summer is queen,
Summer is queen in all the happy land.
Far, far away among the valleys green
Let us go forth and wander hand in hand
Beyond those solemn hills that we have seen
So often welcome home the falling sun
Into their cloudy peaks when day was done-
Beyond them till we find the ocean strand
And hear the great waves run,
With the waste song whose melodies I'd follow
And weary not for many a summer day,
Born of the vaulted breakers arching hollow
Before they flash and scatter into spray,
On, if we should be weary of their play
Then I would lead you further into land
Where, with their ragged walls, the stately rocks
Shunt in smooth courts and paved with quiet sand
To silence dedicate. The sea-god's flocks

Have rested here, and mortal eyes have seen
By great adventure at the dead of noon
A lonely nereid drowsing half a-swoon
Buried beneath her dark and dripping locks.

XVIII. Noon

Noon! and in the garden bower
The hot air quivers o'er the grass,
The little lake is smooth as glass
And still so heavily the hour
Drags, that scarce the proudest flower
Pressed upon its burning bed
Has strength to lift a languid head:
-Rose and fainting violet
By the water's margin set
Swoon and sink as they were dead
Though their weary leaves be fed
With the foam-drops of the pool
Where it trembles dark and cool
Wrinkled by the fountain spraying
O'er it. And the honey-bee
Hums his drowsy melody
And wanders in his course a-straying
Through the sweet and tangled glade
With his golden mead o'erladen,
Where beneath the pleasant shade
Of the darkling boughs a maiden
-Milky limb and fiery tress,
All at sweetest random laid-
Slumbers, drunken with the excess
Of the noontide's loveliness.

XIX. Milton Read Again (In Surrey)

Three golden months while summer on us stole
I have read your joyful tale another time,
Breathing more freely in that larger clime
And learning wiselier to deserve the whole.

Your Spirit, Master, has been close at hand
And guided me, still pointing treasures rare,
Thick-sown where I before saw nothing fair
And finding waters in the barren land,

Barren once thought because my eyes were dim.
Like one I am grown to whom the common field
And often-wandered copse one morning yield
New pleasures suddenly; for over him

Falls the weird spirit of unexplained delight,
New mystery in every shady place,
In every whispering tree a nameless grace,
New rapture on the windy seaward height.

So may she come to me, teaching me well
To savour all these sweets that lie to hand
In wood and lane about this pleasant land
Though it be not the land where I would dwell.

.XX. Sonnet

The stars come out; the fragrant shadows fall
About a dreaming garden still and sweet,
I hear the unseen bats above me bleat
Among the ghostly moths their hunting call,
And twinkling glow-worms all about me crawl.
Now for a chamber dim, a pillow meet
For slumbers deep as death, a faultless sheet,
Cool, white and smooth. So may I reach the hall
With poppies strewn where sleep that is so dear

With magic sponge can wipe away an hour
Or twelve and make them naught. Why not a year,
Why could a man not loiter in that bower
Until a thousand painless cycles wore,
And then-what if it held him evermore?

XXI. The Autumn Morning

See! the pale autumn dawn
Is faint, upon the lawn
That lies in powdered white
Of hoar-frost dight

And now from tree to tree
The ghostly mist we see
Hung like a silver pall
To hallow all.

It wreathes the burdened air
So strangely everywhere
That I could almost fear
This silence drear

Where no one song-bird sings
And dream that wizard things
Mighty for hate or love
Were close above.

White as the fog and fair
Drifting through the middle air
In magic dances dread
Over my head.

Yet these should know me too
Lover and bondman true,
One that has honoured well

The mystic spell

Of earth's most solemn hours
Wherein the ancient powers
Of dryad, elf, or faun
Or leprechaun

Oft have their faces shown
To me that walked alone
Seashore or haunted fen
Or mountain glen

Wherefore I will not fear
To walk the woodlands sere
Into this autumn day
Far, far away.

Part II Hesitation

XXII. L'Apprenti Sorcier

Suddenly there came to me
The music of a mighty sea
That on a bare and iron shore
Thundered with a deeper roar
Than all the tides that leap and run
With us below the real sun:
Because the place was far away,
Above, beyond our homely day,
Neighbouring close the frozen clime
Where out of all the woods of time,
Amid the frightful seraphim
The fierce, cold eyes of Godhead gleam,
Revolving hate and misery
And wars and famines yet to be.
And in my dreams I stood alone

Upon a shelf of weedy stone,
And saw before my shrinking eyes
The dark, enormous breakers rise,
And hover and fall with deafening thunder
Of thwarted foam that echoed under
The ledge, through many a cavern drear,
With hollow sounds of wintry fear.
And through the waters waste and grey,
Thick-strown for many a league away,
Out of the toiling sea arose
Many a face and form of those
Thin, elemental people dear
Who live beyond our heavy sphere.
And all at once from far and near,
They all held out their arms to me,
Crying in their melody,
"Leap in! Leap in and take thy fill
Of all the cosmic good and ill,
Be as the Living ones that know
Enormous joy, enormous woe,
Pain beyond thought and fiery bliss:
For all thy study hunted this,
On wings of magic to arise,
And wash from off thy filmed eyes
The cloud of cold mortality,
To find the real life and be
As are the children of the deep!
Be bold and dare the glorious leap,
Or to thy shame, go, slink again
Back to the narrow ways of men."
So all these mocked me as I stood
Striving to wake because I feared the flood.

XXIII. Alexandrines

There is a house that most of all on earth I hate.

Though I have passed through many sorrows and have been
In bloody fields, sad seas, and countries desolate,
Yet most I fear that empty house where the grasses green
Grow in the silent court the gaping flags between,
And down the moss-grown paths and terrace no man treads
Where the old, old weeds rise deep on the waste garden beds.
Like eyes of one long dead the empty windows stare
And I fear to cross the garden, I fear to linger there,
For in that house I know a little, silent room
Where Someone's always waiting, waiting in the gloom
To draw me with an evil eye, and hold me fast-
Yet thither doom will drive me and He will win at last.

XXIV. In Praise of Solid People

Thank God that there are solid folk
Who water flowers and roll the lawn,
And sit an sew and talk and smoke,
And snore all through the summer dawn.

Who pass untroubled nights and days
Full-fed and sleepily content,
Rejoicing in each other's praise,
Respectable and innocent.

Who feel the things that all men feel,
And think in well-worn grooves of thought,
Whose honest spirits never reel
Before man's mystery, overwrought.

Yet not unfaithful nor unkind,
with work-day virtues surely staid,
Theirs is the sane and humble mind,
And dull affections undismayed.

O happy people! I have seen
No verse yet written in your praise,
And, truth to tell, the time has been
I would have scorned your easy ways.

But now thro' weariness and strife
I learn your worthiness indeed,
The world is better for such life
As stout suburban people lead.

Too often have I sat alone
When the wet night falls heavily,
And fretting winds around me moan,
And homeless longing vexes me

For lore that I shall never know,
And visions none can hope to see,
Till brooding works upon me so
A childish fear steals over me.

I look around the empty room,
The clock still ticking in its place,
And all else silent as the tomb,
Till suddenly, I think, a face

Grows from the darkness just beside.
I turn, and lo! it fades away,
And soon another phantom tide
Of shifting dreams begins to play,

And dusky galleys past me sail,
Full freighted on a faerie sea;
I hear the silken merchants hail
Across the ringing waves to me

-Then suddenly, again, the room,

Familiar books about me piled,
And I alone amid the gloom,
By one more mocking dream beguiled.

And still no neared to the Light,
And still no further from myself,
Alone and lost in clinging night
-(The clock's still ticking on the shelf).

Then do I envy solid folk
Who sit of evenings by the fire,
After their work and doze and smoke,
And are not fretted by desire.

Part III The Escape

XXV. Song of the Pilgrims

O Dwellers at the back of the North Wind,
What have we done to you? How have we sinned
Wandering the Earth from Orkney unto Ind?

With many deaths our fellowship is thinned,
Our flesh is withered in the parching wind,
Wandering the earth from Orkney unto Ind.

We have no rest. We cannot turn again
Back to the world and all her fruitless pain,
Having once sought the land where ye remain.

Some say ye are not. But, ah God! we know
That somewhere, somewhere past the Northern snow
Waiting for us the red-rose gardens blow:

-The red-rose and the white-rose gardens blow
In the green Northern land to which we go,

Surely the ways are long and the years are slow.

We have forsaken all things sweet and fair,
We have found nothing worth a moment's care
Because the real flowers are blowing there.

Land of the Lotus fallen from the sun,
Land of the Lake from whence all rivers run,
Land where the hope of all our dreams is won!

Shall we not somewhere see at close of day
The green walls of that country far away,
And hear the music of her fountains play?

So long we have been wandering all this while
By many a perilous sea and drifting isle,
We scarce shall dare to look thereon and smile.

Yea, when we are drawing very near to thee,
And when at last the ivory port we see
Our hearts will faint with mere felicity:

But we shall wake again in gardens bright
Of green and gold for infinite delight,
Sleeping beneath the solemn mountains white,
While from the flowery copses still unseen
Sing out the crooning birds that ne'er have been
Touched by the hand of winter frore and lean;

And ever living queens that grow not old
And poets wise in robes of faerie gold
Whisper a wild, sweet song that first was told

Ere God sat down to make the Milky Way.
And in those gardens we shall sleep and play
For ever and for ever and a day.

Ah, Dwellers at the back of the North Wind,
What have we done to you? How have we sinned,
That yes should hide beyond the Northern wind?

Land of the Lotus, fallen from the Sun,
When shall your hidden, flowery vales be won
And all the travail of our way be done?

Very far we have searched; we have even seen
The Scythian waste that bears no soft nor green,
And near the Hideous Pass our feet have been.

We have heard Syrens singing all night long
Beneath the unknown stars their lonely song
In friendless seas beyond the Pillars strong.

Nor by the dragon-daughter of Hypocras
Nor the vale of the Devil's head we have feared to pass,
Yet is our labour lost and vain, alas!

Scouring the earth from Orkney unto Ind,
Tossed on the seas and withered in the wind,
We seek and seek your land. How have we sinned?

Or is it all a folly of the wise,
Bidding us walk these ways with blinded eyes
While all around us real flowers arise?

But, by the very God, we know, we know
That somewhere still, beyond the Northern snow
Waiting for us the red-rose gardens blow.

XXVI. Song

Faeries must be in the woods

Or the satyrs' laughing broods-
Tritons in the summer sea,
Else how could the dead things be
Half so lovely as they are?
How could wealth of star on star
Dusted o'er the frosty night
Fill thy spirit with delight
And lead thee from this care of thine
Up among the dreams divine,
Were it not that each and all
Of them that walk the heavenly hall
Is in truth a happy isle,
Where eternal meadows smile,
And golden globes of fruit are seen
Twinkling through the orchards green;
Were the Other People go
On the bright sward to and fro?
Atoms dead could never thus
Stir the human heart of us
Unless the beauty that we see
The veil of endless beauty be,
Filled full of spirits that have trod
Far hence along the heavenly sod
And see the bright footprints of God.

XXVII. The Ass

I woke and rose and slipt away
To the heathery hills in the morning grey.

In a field where the dew lay cold and deep
I met an ass, new-roused from sleep.

I stroked his nose and I tickled his ears,
And spoke soft words to quiet his fears.

His eyes stared into the eyes of me
And he kissed my hands of his courtesy.

"O big, brown brother out of the waste,
How do thistles for breakfast taste?

"And do you rejoice in the dawn divine
With a heart that is glad no less than mine?

"For, brother, the depth of your gentle eyes
Is strange and mystic as the skies:

"What are the thoughts that grope behind,
Down in the mist of a donkey mind?

"Can it be true, as the wise men tell,
That you are a mask of God as well,

"And, as in us, so in you no less
Speaks the eternal Loveliness,

"And words of the lips that all things know
Among the thoughts of a donkey go?

"However it be, O four-foot brother,
Fair to-day is the earth, our mother.

"God send you peace and delight thereof,
And all green meat of the waste you love,

"And guard you well from violent men
Who'd put you back in the shafts again."

But the ass had far too wise a head
To answer one of the things I said,

So he twitched his fair ears up and down
And turned to nuzzle his shoulder brown.

XXVIII. Ballade Mystique

The big, red-house is bare and lone
The stony garden waste and sere
With blight of breezes ocean blown
To pinch the wakening of the year;
My kindly friends with busy cheer
My wretchedness could plainly show.
They tell me I am lonely here-
What do they know? What do they know?
They think that while the gables moan
And easements creak in winter drear
I should be piteously alone
Without the speech of comrades dear;
And friendly for my sake they fear,
It grieves them thinking of me so
While all their happy life is near-
What do they know? What do they know?

That I have seen the Dagda's throne
In sunny lands without a tear
And found a forest all my own
To ward with magic shield and spear,
Where, through the stately towers I rear
For my desire, around me go
Immortal shapes of beauty clear:
They do not know, they do not know.

L'Envoi

The friends I have without a peer
Beyond the western ocean's glow,
Whither the faerie galleys steer,

They do not know: how should they know?

XXIX. Night

I know a little Druid wood
Where I would slumber if I could
And have the murmuring of the stream
To mingle with a midnight dream,
And have the holy hazel trees
To play above me in the breeze,
And smell the thorny eglantine;
For there the white owls all night long
In the scented gloom divine
Hear the wild, strange, tuneless song
Of faerie voices, thin and high
As the bat's unearthly cry,
And the measure of their shoon
Dancing, dancing, under the moon,
Until, amid the pale of dawn
The wandering stars begin to swoon. . . .
Ah, leave the world and come away!

The windy folk are in the glade,
And men have seen their revels, laid
In secret on some flowery lawn
Underneath the beechen covers,
Kings of old, I've heard them say,
Here have found them faerie lovers
That charmed them out of life and kissed
Their lips with cold lips unafraid,
And such a spell around them made
That they have passed beyond the mist
And found the Country-under-wave. . . .

Kings of old, whom none could save!

XXX. Oxford

It is well that there are palaces of peace
And discipline and dreaming and desire,
Lest we forget our heritage and cease
The Spirit's work-to hunger and aspire:

Lest we forget that we were born divine,
Now tangled in red battle's animal net,
Murder the work and lust the anodyne,
Pains of the beast 'gainst bestial solace set.

But this shall never be: to us remains
One city that has nothing of the beast,
That was not built for gross, material gains,
Sharp, wolfish power or empire's glutted feast.

We are not wholly brute. To us remains
A clean, sweet city lulled by ancient streams,
A place of visions and of loosening chains,
A refuge of the elect, a tower of dreams.

She was not builded out of common stone
But out of all men's yearning and all prayer
That she might live, eternally our own,
The Spirit's stronghold-barred against despair.

XXXI. Hymn (For Boys' Voices)

All the things magicians do
Could be done by me and you
Freely, if we only knew.

Human children every day
Could play at games the faeries play
If they were but shown the way.

Every man a God would be
Laughing through eternity
If as God's his eyes could see.

All the wizardries of God-
Slaying matter with a nod,
Charming spirits with his rod,

With the singing of his voice
Making lonely lands rejoice,
Leaving us no will nor choice,

Drawing headlong me and you
As the piping Orpheus drew
Man and beast the mountains through,

By the sweetness of his horn
Calling us from lands forlorn
Nearer to the widening morn-

All that loveliness of power
Could be man's peculiar dower,
Even mine, this very hour;

We should reach the Hidden Land
And grow immortal out of hand,
If we could but understand!

We could revel day and night
In all power and all delight
If we learn to think aright.

XXXII. "Our Daily Bread"

We need no barbarous words nor solemn spell

To raise the unknown. It lies before our feet;
There have been men who sank down into Hell
In some suburban street,

And some there are that in their daily walks
Have met archangels fresh from sight of God,
Or watched how in their beans and cabbage-stalks
Long files of faerie trod.

Often me too the Living voices call
In many a vulgar and habitual place,
I catch a sight of lands beyond the wall,
I see a strange god's face.

And some day this work will work upon me so
I shall arise and leave both friends and home
And over many lands a pilgrim go
Through alien woods and foam,

Seeking the last steep edges of the earth
Whence I may leap into that gulf of light
Wherein, before my narrowing Self had birth,
Part of me lived aright.

XXXIII. How He Saw Angus the God

I heard the swallow sing in the eaves and rose
All in a strange delight while others slept,
And down the creaking stair, alone, tip-toes,
So carefully I crept.

The house was dark with silly blinds yet drawn,
But outside the clean air was filled with light,
And underneath my feet the cold, wet lawn
With dew was twinkling bright.

The cobwebs hung from every branch and spray
Gleaming with pearly strands of laden thread,
And long and still the morning shadows lay
Across the meadows spread.

At that pure hour when yet no sound of man,
Stirs in the whiteness of the wakening earth,
Alone through innocent solitudes I ran
Singing aloud for mirth.

Till I had found the open mountain heath
Yellow with gorse, and rested there and stood
To gaze upon the misty sea beneath,
Or on the neighbouring wood,

-That little wood of hazel and tall pine
And youngling fir, where oft we have loved to see
The level beams of early morning shine
Freshly from tree to tree.
Through the denser wood there's many a pool
Of deep and night-born shadow lingers yet
Where the new-wakened flowers are damp and cool
And the long grass is wet.

In the sweet heather long I rested there
Looking upon the dappled, early sky,
When suddenly, from out the shining air
A god came flashing by.

Swift, naked, eager, pitilessly fair,
With a live crown of birds about his head,
Singing and fluttering, and his fiery hair,
Far out behind him spread,

Streamed like a rippling torch upon the breeze
Of his own glorious swiftness: in the grass

He bruised no feathery stalk, and through the trees
I saw his whiteness pass.

But when I followed him beyond the wood,
Lo! He was changed into a solemn bull
That there upon the open pasture stood
And browsed his lazy full.

XXXIV. The Roads

I stand on the windy uplands among the hills of Down
With all the world spread out beneath, meadow and sea and town,
And ploughlands on the far-off hills that glow with friendly brown.

And ever across the rolling land to the far horizon line,
Where the blue hills border the misty west, I see the white roads twine,
The rare roads and the fair roads that call this heart of mine.

I see them dip in the valleys and vanish and rise and bend
From shadowy dell to windswept fell, and still to the West they wend,
And over the cold blue ridge at last to the great world's uttermost end.

And the call of the roads is upon me, a desire in my spirit has grown
To wander forth in the highways, 'twixt earth and sky alone,
And seek for the lands no foot has trod and the seas no sail has known:

For the lands to the west of the evening and east of the morning's birth,

Where the gods unseen in their valleys green are glad at the ends of the earth
And fear no morrow to bring them sorrow, nor night to quench their mirth.

XXXV. Hesperus

Through the starry hollow
Of the summer night
I would follow, follow
Hesperus the bright,
To seek beyond the western wave
His garden of delight.

Hesperus the fairest
Of all gods that are,
Peace and dreams thou bearest
In thy shadowy car,
And often in my evening walks
I've blessed thee from afar.

Stars without number,
Dust the noon of night,
Thou the early slumber
And the still delight
Of the gentle twilit hours
Rulest in thy right.

When the pale skies shiver,
Seeing night is done,
Past the ocean-river,
Lightly thou dost run,
To look for pleasant, sleepy lands,
That never fear the sun.

Where, beyond the waters
Of the outer sea,

Thy triple crown of daughters
That guards the golden tree
Sing out across the lonely tide
A welcome home to thee.

And while the old, old dragon
For joy lifts up his head,
They bring thee forth a flagon
Of nectar foaming red,
And underneath the drowsy trees
Of poppies strew thy bed.

Ah! that I could follow
In thy footsteps bright,
Through the starry hollow
Of the summer night,
Sloping down the western ways
To find my heart's delight!

XXXVI. The Star Bath

A place uplifted towards the midnight sky
Far, far away among the mountains old,
A treeless waste of rocks and freezing cold,
Where the dead, cheerless moon rode neighbouring by-
And in the midst a silent tarn there lay,
A narrow pool, cold as the tide that flows
Where monstrous bergs beyond Varanger stray,
Rising from sunless depths that no man knows;
Thither as clustering fireflies have I seen
At fixed seasons all the stars come down
To wash in that cold wave their brightness clean
And win the special fire wherewith they crown
The wintry heavens in frost. Even as a flock
Of falling birds, down to the pool they came.
I saw them and I heard the icy shock

Of stars engulfed with hissing of faint flame
-Ages ago before the birth of men
Or earliest beast. Yet I was still the same
That now remember, knowing not where or when.

XXXVII. Tu Ne Quaesieris

For all the lore of Lodge and Myers
I cannot heal my torn desires,
Nor hope for all that man can speer
To make the riddling earth grow clear.
Though it were sure and proven well
That I shall prosper, as they tell,
In fields beneath a different sun
By shores where other oceans run,
When this live body that was I
Lies hidden from the cheerful sky,
Yet what were endless lives to me
If still my narrow self I be
And hope and fail and struggle still,
And break my will against God's will,
To play for stakes of pleasure and pain
And hope and fail and hope again,
Deluded, thwarted, striving elf
That through the window of my self
As through a dark glass scarce can see
A warped and masked reality?
But when this searching thought of mine
Is mingled in the large Divine,
And laughter that was in my mouth
Runs through the breezes of the South,
When glory I have built in dreams
Along some fiery sunset gleams,
And my dead sin and foolishness
Grow one with Nature's whole distress,
To perfect being I shall win,

And where I end will Life begin.

XXXVIII. Lullaby

Lullaby! Lullaby!
There's a tower strong and high
Built of oak and brick and stone,
Stands before a wood alone.
The doors are of the oak so brown
As any ale in Oxford town,
The walls are builded warm and thick
Of the old red Roman brick,
The good grey stone is over all
In arch and floor of the tower tall.
And maidens three are living there
All in the upper chamber fair,
Hung with silver, hung with pall,
And stories painted on the wall.
And softly goes the whirring loom
In my ladies' upper room,
For they shall spin both night and day
Until the stars do pass away.
But every night at evening.
The window open wide they fling,
And one of them says a word they know
And out as three white swans they go,
And the murmuring of the woods is drowned
In the soft wings' whirring sound,
As they go flying round, around,
Singing in swans' voices high
A lonely, lovely lullaby.

XXXIX. World's Desire

Love, there is a castle built in a country desolate,
On a rock above a forest where the trees are grim and great,

Blasted with the lightning sharp-giant boulders strewn between,
And the mountains rise above, and the cold ravine
Echoes to the crushing roar and thunder of a mighty river
Raging down a cataract. Very tower and forest quiver
And the grey wolves are afraid and the call of birds is drowned,
And the thought and speech of man in the boiling water's sound.
But upon the further side of the barren, sharp ravine
With the sunlight on its turrets is the castle seen,
Calm and very wonderful, white above the green
Of the wet and waving forest, slanted all away,
Because the driving Northern wind will not rest by night or day.
Yet the towers are sure above, very mighty is the stead,
The gates are made of ivory, the roofs of copper red.

Round and round the warders grave walk upon the walls for ever
And the wakeful dragons couch in the ports of ivory,
Nothing is can trouble it, hate of the gods nor man's endeavour,
And it shall be a resting-place, dear heart, for you and me.

Through the wet and waving forest with an age-old sorrow laden
Singing of the world's regret wanders wild the faerie maiden,
Through the thistle and the brier, through the tangles of the thorn,
Till her eyes be dim with weeping and her homeless feet are torn.

Often to the castle gate up she looks with vain endeavour,
For her soulless loveliness to the castle winneth never.

But within the sacred court, hidden high upon the mountain,
Wandering in the castle gardens lovely folk enough there be,
Breathing in another air, drinking of a purer fountain
And among that folk, beloved, there's a place for you and me.

XL. Death in Battle

Open the gates for me,
Open the gates of the peaceful castle, rosy in the West,
In the sweet dim Isle of Apples over the wide sea's breast,

Open the gates for me!

Sorely pressed have I been
And driven and hurt beyond bearing this summer day,
But the heat and the pain together suddenly fall away,
All's cool and green.

But a moment agone,
Among men cursing in fight and toiling, blinded I fought,
But the labour passed on a sudden even as a passing thought,

And now—alone!

Ah, to be ever alone,
In flowery valleys among the mountains and silent wastes untrod,
In the dewy upland places, in the garden of God,
This would atone!

I shall not see

The brutal, crowded faces around me, that in their toil have grown
Into the faces of devils-yea, even as my own-
When I find thee,

O Country of Dreams!
Beyond the tide of the ocean, hidden and sunk away,
Out of the sound of battles, near to the end of day,
Full of dim woods and streams.
C S Lewis (Clive Hamilton)

Wordsworth

"That best portion of a man's life, his little, nameless, unremembered acts of kindness and love."

Gracious Spirit, Holy Ghost

Gracious Spirit, Holy Ghost,
taught by You, we covet most,
of Your gifts at Pentecost,
holy, heavenly love.
Faith that mountains could remove,
tongues of earth or heaven above,
knowledge, all things, empty prove
without heavenly love.
Though I as a martyr bleed,
give my goods the poor to feed,
all is vain if love I need;
therefore give me love.
Love is kind, and suffers long;
love is meek, and thinks no wrong;
love, than death itself more strong:
therefore give us love.
Prophecy will fade away,
melting in the light of day;
love will ever with us stay:
therefore give us love.
Faith, and hope, and love we see
joining hand in hand, agree;
but the greatest of the three,
and the best, is love.

O Lord of Heaven and Earth and Sea

O Lord of heaven and earth and sea,
to thee all praise and glory be;
how shall we show our love to thee,
who givest all?
The golden sunshine, vernal air,
sweet flowers and fruits, thy love declare;
where harvests ripen, thou art there,
who givest all.
For peaceful homes and healthful days,
for all the blessings earth displays,
we owe thee thankfulness and praise,
who givest all.
Thou didst not spare thine only Son,
but gav'st him for a world undone,
and freely, with that blessèd One,
thou givest all.
Thou giv'st the Spirit's blessèd dower,
Spirit of life and love and power,
and dost his sevenfold graces shower
upon us all.
For souls redeemed, for sins forgiven,
for means of grace and hopes of heaven,
Father, all praise to thee be given,
who givest all.
We lose what on ourselves we spend,
we have as treasure without end
whatever, Lord, to thee we lend,
who givest all.
To thee, from whom we all derive
our life, our gifts, our power to give:
O may we ever with thee live,
who givest all.

Songs of Thankfulness and Praise

Songs of thankfulness and praise Jesus, Lord, to you we raise,
God revealed by guiding star to the sages from afar,
Branch of royal David's stem, in your birth at Bethlehem:
Anthems be to you addressed, God in Christ made manifest.
God revealed at Jordan's stream, God's beloved Son supreme,
And at Cana, wedding guest, in your power manifest,
God revealed in works divine, changing water into wine:
Anthems be to you addressed, God in Christ made manifest.
God revealed in making whole weakened limbs and fainting soul,
God revealed in valiant fight quelling all the devil's might,
God revealed in gracious will, ever bringing good from ill:
Anthems be to you addressed, God in Christ made manifest.
Manifest on mountain height, shining in resplendent light,
Where disciples filled with awe your transfigured glory saw;
From that place you went with them steadfast to Jerusalem;
Cross and Easter day attest, God in Christ made manifest.
Grant us grace to see you, Lord, mirrored in your holy word;
May we imitate you still and obey your perfect will,
That we like to you may be, at your great Epiphany:
May your glory be confessed, God in Christ made manifest.

Emily Dickinson

"They say that God is everywhere, and yet we always think of Him as somewhat of a recluse."

Tie the strings to my life, my Lord

Tie the strings to my life, my Lord,
Then I am ready to go!
Just a look at the horses--
Rapid! That will do!

Put me in on the firmest side,
So I shall never fall;
For we must ride to the Judgment,
And it's partly down hill.

But never I mind the bridges,
And never I mind the sea;
Held fast in everlasting race
By my own choice and thee.

Good-by to the life I used to live,
And the world I used to know;
And kiss the hills for me, just once;
Now I am ready to go!

The Chariot

Because I could not stop for Death,
He kindly stopped for me;
The carriage held but just ourselves
And Immortality.

We slowly drove, he knew no haste,
And I had put away
My labor, and my leisure too,
For his civility

We passed the school where children played,
Their lessons scarcely done;
We passed the fields of gazing grain,
We passed the setting sun.

We paused before a house that seemed
A swelling of the ground;
The roof was scarcely visible
The cornice but a mound.

Since then 'tis centuries; but each
Feels shorter than the day
I first surmised the horses' heads
Were toward eternity.

Safe in their alabaster chambers

Safe in their alabaster chambers,
Untouched by morning and untouched by noon,
Sleep the meek members of the resurrection.
Rafter of satin, and roof of stone.

Light laughs the breeze in her castle of sunshine;
Babbles the bee in a stolid ear;
Pipe the sweet birds in ignorant cadence,--
Ah, what sagacity perished here!

Grand go the years in the crescent above them;
Worlds scoop their arcs, and firmaments row,
Diadems drop and Doges surrender,
Soundless as dots on a disk of snow.

3.
The Musical Poets

Psalms 146: "***1*** *Praise ye the LORD. Praise the LORD, O my soul.* ***2*** *While I live will I praise the LORD: I will sing praises unto my God while I have any being.* ***3*** *Put not your trust in princes, nor in the son of man, in whom there is no help.* ***4*** *His breath goeth forth , he returneth to his earth; in that very day his thoughts perish .* ***5*** *Happy is he that hath the God of Jacob for his help, whose hope is in the LORD his God:* ***6*** *Which made heaven, and earth, the sea, and all that therein is: which keepeth truth for ever:* ***7*** *Which executeth judgment for the oppressed : which giveth food to the hungry. The LORD looseth the prisoners :* ***8*** *The LORD openeth the eyes of the blind: the LORD raiseth them that are bowed down : the LORD loveth the righteous:* ***9*** *The LORD preserveth the strangers; he relieveth the fatherless and widow: but the way of the wicked he turneth upside down .* ***10*** *The LORD shall reign for ever, even thy God, O Zion, unto all generations. Praise ye the LORD.*"

Sarah F. Adams

"O Love! thou makest all things even
In earth or heaven;
Finding thy way through prison-bars
Up to the stars;
Or, true to the Almighty plan,
That out of dust created man,
Thou lookest in a grave,--to see
Thine immortality!"

Nearer, My God, to Thee

Nearer, my God, to Thee, nearer to Thee!
E'en though it be a cross that raiseth me,
Still all my song shall be, nearer, my God, to Thee.
Nearer, my God, to Thee, nearer to Thee!
Though like the wanderer, the sun gone down,
Darkness be over me, my rest a stone;
Yet in my dreams I'd be nearer, my God, to Thee.
Nearer, my God, to Thee, nearer to Thee!
There let the way appear, steps unto Heav'n;
All that Thou sendest me, in mercy giv'n;
Angels to beckon me nearer, my God, to Thee.
Nearer, my God, to Thee, nearer to Thee!
Then, with my waking thoughts bright with Thy praise,
Out of my stony griefs Bethel I'll raise;
So by my woes to be nearer, my God, to Thee.
Nearer, my God, to Thee, nearer to Thee!
Or, if on joyful wing cleaving the sky,
Sun, moon, and stars forgot, upward I'll fly,
Still all my song shall be, nearer, my God, to Thee.
Nearer, my God, to Thee, nearer to Thee!
There in my Father's home, safe and at rest,
There in my Savior's love, perfectly blest;
Age after age to be nearer, my God, to Thee.
Nearer, my God, to Thee, nearer to Thee!

Fanny J. Crosby

"When I get to heaven, the first face that shall ever gladden my sight will be that of my Savior."

Blessed Assurance

Blessed assurance, Jesus is mine!
O what a foretaste of glory divine!
Heir of salvation, purchase of God,
Born of His Spirit, washed in His blood.
Perfect submission, perfect delight!
Visions of rapture now burst on my sight;
Angels descending bring from above
Echoes of mercy, whispers of love.
Perfect submission, all is at rest!
I in my Savior am happy and blest,
Watching and waiting, looking above,
Filled with his goodness, lost in His love.
This is my story, this is my song,
praising my Savior all the day long;
this is my story, this is my song,
praising my Savior all the day long.

Holy, Holy, Holy is the Lord

Holy, holy, holy is the Lord!
Sing, O ye people, gladly adore Him;
Let the mountains tremble at His word;
Let the hills be joyful before Him;
Mighty in wisdom, boundless in mercy,
Great is Jehovah, King over all.
Praise Him, praise Him! shout aloud for joy,
Watchman of Zion, herald the story;
Sin and death His kingdom shall destroy;
All the earth shall sing of His glory;
Praise Him, ye angels, ye who behold Him,
Robed in His splendor, matchless, divine.
King eternal, blessèd be His Name!
So may His children gladly adore Him;
When in Heav'n we join the happy strain,
When we cast our bright crowns before Him;
There in His likeness joyful awaking,
There we shall see Him, there we shall sing:
Holy, holy, holy is the Lord!
Let the hills be joyful before Him.

To God Be the Glory

To God be the glory,
Great things He hath done;
So loved He the world
That He gave us His Son,
Who yielded His life
An atonement for sin,
And opened the lifegate
That all may go in.
O perfect redemption,
The purchase of blood,
To ev'ry believer
The promise of God;
The vilest offender
Who truly believes,
That moment from Jesus
A pardon receives.
Great things He hath taught us,
Great things He hath done,
And great our rejoicing
Thro' Jesus the Son;
But purer, and higher,
And greater will be
Our wonder, our vict'ry
When Jesus we see.
Praise the Lord, praise the Lord,
Let the earth hear His Voice!
Praise the Lord, praise the Lord,
Let the people rejoice!
O come to the Father
Thro' Jesus the Son,
And give Him the glory,
Great things He hath done.

Charles Wesley

"Do all the good you can, By all the means you can,
In all the ways you can, In all the places you can,
At all the times you can, To all the people you can
As long as ever you can!"

O For a Thousand Tongues to Sing

O for a thousand tongues to sing
My great Redeemer's praise,
The glories of my God and King,
The triumphs of His grace!
My gracious Master and my God,
Assist me to proclaim,
To spread through all the earth abroad
The honors of Thy name.
Jesus! the name that charms our fears,
That bids our sorrows cease;
'Tis music in the sinner's ears,
'Tis life, and health, and peace.
He breaks the power of canceled sin,
He sets the prisoner free;
His blood can make the foulest clean,
His blood availed for me.
He speaks, and, listening to His voice,
New life the dead receive,
The mournful, broken hearts rejoice,
The humble poor believe.
Hear Him, ye deaf; His praise, ye dumb,
Your loosened tongues employ;
Ye blind, behold your Savior come,
And leap, ye lame, for joy.
In Christ your Head, you then shall know,
Shall feel your sins forgiven;
Anticipate your heaven below,
And own that love is heaven.
Glory to God, and praise and love
Be ever, ever given,
By saints below and saints above,
The church in earth and heaven.
On this glad day the glorious Sun
Of Righteousness arose;

On my benighted soul He shone
And filled it with repose.
Sudden expired the legal strife,
'Twas then I ceased to grieve;
My second, real, living life
I then began to live.
Then with my heart I first believed,
Believed with faith divine,
Power with the Holy Ghost received
To call the Savior mine.
I felt my Lord's atoning blood
Close to my soul applied;
Me, me He loved, the Son of God,
For me, for me He died!
I found and owned His promise true,
Ascertained of my part,
My pardon passed in heaven I knew
When written on my heart.
Look unto Him, ye nations, own
Your God, ye fallen race;
Look, and be saved through faith alone,
Be justified by grace.
See all your sins on Jesus laid:
The Lamb of God was slain,
His soul was once an offering made
For every soul of man.
Awake from guilty nature's sleep,
And Christ shall give you light,
Cast all your sins into the deep,
And wash the Æthiop white.
Harlots and publicans and thieves
In holy triumph join!
Saved is the sinner that believes
From crimes as great as mine.
Murderers and all ye hellish crew
In holy triumph join!

Believe the Savior died for you;
For me the Savior died.
With me, your chief, ye then shall know,
Shall feel your sins forgiven;
Anticipate your heaven below,
And own that love is heaven.

Jesus, Lover of My Soul

Jesus, lover of my soul, let me to Thy bosom fly,
While the nearer waters roll, while the tempest still is high.
Hide me, O my Savior, hide, till the storm of life is past;
Safe into the haven guide; O receive my soul at last.
Other refuge have I none, hangs my helpless soul on Thee;
Leave, ah! leave me not alone, still support and comfort me.
All my trust on Thee is stayed, all my help from Thee I bring;
Cover my defenseless head with the shadow of Thy wing.
Wilt Thou not regard my call? Wilt Thou not accept my prayer?
Lo! I sink, I faint, I fall—Lo! on Thee I cast my care;
Reach me out Thy gracious hand! While I of Thy strength receive,
Hoping against hope I stand, dying, and behold, I live.
Thou, O Christ, art all I want, more than all in Thee I find;
Raise the fallen, cheer the faint, heal the sick, and lead the blind.
Just and holy is Thy Name, I am all unrighteousness;
False and full of sin I am; Thou art full of truth and grace.
Plenteous grace with Thee is found, grace to cover all my sin;
Let the healing streams abound; make and keep me pure within.
Thou of life the fountain art, freely let me take of Thee;
Spring Thou up within my heart; rise to all eternity

John Newton

"I am not what I ought to be, I am not what I want to be, I am not what I hope to be in another world; but still I am not what I once used to be, and by the grace of God I am what I am"

Amazing Grace

Amazing grace! How sweet the sound
That saved a wretch like me!
I once was lost, but now am found;
Was blind, but now I see.
'Twas grace that taught my heart to fear,
And grace my fears relieved;
How precious did that grace appear
The hour I first believed!
Through many dangers, toils and snares,
I have already come;
'Tis grace hath brought me safe thus far,
And grace will lead me home.
The Lord has promised good to me,
His Word my hope secures;
He will my Shield and Portion be,
As long as life endures.
Yea, when this flesh and heart shall fail,
And mortal life shall cease,
I shall possess, within the veil,
A life of joy and peace.
The earth shall soon dissolve like snow,
The sun forbear to shine;
But God, who called me here below,
Will be forever mine.
When we've been there ten thousand years,
Bright shining as the sun,
We've no less days to sing God's praise
Than when we'd first begun.

Approach, My Soul, the Mercy Seat

Approach, my soul, the mercy seat,
Where Jesus answers prayer;
There humbly fall before His feet,
For none can perish there.
Thy promise is my only plea,
With this I venture nigh;
Thou callest burdened souls to Thee,
And such, O Lord, am I.
Bowed down beneath a load of sin,
By Satan sorely pressed,
By war without and fears within,
I come to Thee for rest.
Be Thou my Shield and hiding Place,
That, sheltered by Thy side,
I may my fierce accuser face,
And tell him Thou hast died!
O wondrous love! to bleed and die,
To bear the cross and shame,
That guilty sinners, such as I,
Might plead Thy gracious Name.
"Poor tempest-tossèd soul, be still;
My promised grace receive";
'Tis Jesus speaks—I must, I will,
I can, I do believe.

Dear Shepherd of thy People, Hear

Dear Shepherd of Thy people, hear;
Thy presence now display;
As Thou hast given a place for prayer,
So give us hearts to pray.
O Lord, our languid souls inspire,
For here, we trust, thou art!
Send down a coal of heav'nly fire,
To warm each waiting heart.
Show us some token of Thy love,
Our fainting hope to raise;
And pour Thy blessings from above,
That we may render praise.
Within these walls let holy peace
And love and concord dwell;
Here give the troubled conscience ease,
The wounded spirit heal.
The feeling heart, the melting eye,
The humble mind bestow;
And shine upon us from on high,
To make our graces grow!
May we in faith receive Thy Word,
In faith present our prayers;
And, in the presence of our Lord,
Unbosom all our cares.
And may the Gospel's joyful sound
Enforced by mighty grace,
Awaken many sinners round,
To come and fill the place.

How Sweet the Name of Jesus Sounds

How sweet the Name of Jesus sounds
In a believer's ear!
It soothes his sorrows, heals his wounds,
And drives away his fear.
It makes the wounded spirit whole,
And calms the troubled breast;
'Tis manna to the hungry soul,
And to the weary, rest.
Dear Name, the Rock on which I build,
My Shield and Hiding Place,
My never failing treasury, filled
With boundless stores of grace!
By Thee my prayers acceptance gain,
Although with sin defiled;
Satan accuses me in vain,
And I am owned a child.
Jesus! my Shepherd, Husband, Friend,
O Prophet, Priest and King,
My Lord, my Life, my Way, my End,
Accept the praise I bring.
Weak is the effort of my heart,
And cold my warmest thought;
But when I see Thee as Thou art,
I'll praise Thee as I ought.
Till then I would Thy love proclaim
With every fleeting breath,
And may the music of Thy Name
Refresh my soul in death!

Ambrose of Milan

"Perhaps you say, Why are the wicked joyous? Why do they live in luxury? Why do they not toil with me? It is because they who have not put down their names to strive for the crown are not bound to undergo the labors of the contest. They who have not gone down into the race-course do not anoint themselves with oil nor get covered with dust. For those whom glory awaits trouble is at hand. The perfumed spectators are wont to look on, not to join in the struggle, nor to endure the sun, the heat, the dust, and the showers ..."

Now That the Daylight Fills the Sky

Now that the daylight fills the sky,
We lift our hearts to God on high,
That He, in all we do or say,
Would keep us free from harm today.
May He restrain our tongues from strife,
And shield from anger's din our life,
And guard with watchful care our eyes
From earth's absorbing vanities.
O may our inmost hearts be pure,
From thoughts of folly kept secure,
And pride of sinful flesh subdued
Through sparing use of daily food.
So we, when this day's work is o'er,
And shades of night return once more,
Our path of trial safely trod,
Shall give the glory to our God.
All praise to God the Father be,
All praise, eternal Son, to Thee,
Whom with the Spirit we adore
Forever and forevermore.

O Splendor of God's Glory Bright

O splendor of God's glory bright,
From light eternal bringing light,
Thou Light of light, light's living Spring,
True Day, all days illumining.
Come, very Sun of Heaven's love,
In lasting radiance from above,
And pour the Holy Spirit's ray
On all we think or do today.
And now to Thee our pray'rs ascend,
O Father glorious without end;
We plead with Sovereign Grace for pow'r
To conquer in temptation's hour.
Confirm our will to do the right,
And keep our hearts from envy's blight;
Let faith her eager fires renew,
And hate the false, and love the true.
O joyful be the passing day
With thoughts as pure as morning's ray,
With faith like noontide shining bright,
Our souls unshadowed by the night.
Dawn's glory gilds the earth and skies,
Let Him, our prefect Morn, arise,
The Word in God the Father one,
The Father imaged by the Son.

Ephrem the Syrian

"Let books be your dining table, / And you shall be full of delights. / Let them be your mattress,/And you shall sleep restful nights"

Get Up My Soul Arise

Get up my soul arise
You have slept till now in sin
Shake off your slumber hurry
Seek refuge in the Just One

Seek him in repentance
He may be moved to mercy
Put off the veil of corruption
That your eye might rightly see

You who forgives sins
And freely grants mercy
With the Prodigals who repent
I will gather and exalt Thee

With passions like a storm
A ship drowned on the sea
My thoughts are like thorns
And bear no fruit on the tree

Heal my wounds with tears
This soul withdrawn from Thee
At your righteous judgment
May your compassion shelter me

_Adapted by Eddy Duhan

I Run To You With Love

My soul is choked by sorrow
I stand before you with tears
Regard me and I will be saved
Heal me of my wasted years

I run to you with love
Lord I run to you with love

Deliver me from the enemy
Who is a rival for my soul
There is no other God but Thee
And no other good I can recall

I run to you with love
Lord I run to you with love

Immortal and jealous God
I approach you without shame
For I am betrothed to you
You have given me your name

I run to you with love
Lord I run to you with love

_Adapted by Eddy Duhan

James Weldon Johnson

"Labor is the fabled magician's wand, the philosophers stone, and the cap of good fortune."

Lift ev'ry voice and Sing

Lift ev'ry voice and sing,
Till earth and heaven ring,
Ring with the harmonies of Liberty;
Let our rejoicing rise
High as the list'ning skies,
Let it resound loud as the rolling sea.
Sing a song full of the faith that the dark past has taught us,
Sing a song full of the hope that the present has brought us;
Facing the rising sun of our new day begun,
Let us march on till victory is won.

Stony the road we trod,
Bitter the chast'ning rod,
Felt in the days when hope unborn had died;
Yet with a steady beat,
Have not our weary feet
Come to the place for which our fathers sighed?
We have come over a way that with tears has been watered.
We have come, treading our path through the blood of the slaughtered,
Out from the gloomy past,
Till now we stand at last
Where the white gleam of our bright star is cast.

God of our weary years,
God of our silent tears,
Thou who hast brought us thus far on the way;
Thou who hast by Thy might,
Led us into the light,
Keep us forever in the path, we pray.
Lest our feet stray from the places, our God, where we met Thee,
Lest our hearts, drunk with the wine of the world, we forget Thee;

Shadowed beneath Thy hand,
May we forever stand,
True to our God,
True to our native land.

Go Down Death

Weep not, weep not,
She is not dead;
She's resting in the bosom of Jesus.
Heart-broken husband–weep no more;
Grief-stricken son–weep no more;
Left-lonesome daughter –weep no more;
She only just gone home.
Day before yesterday morning,
God was looking down from his great, high heaven,
Looking down on all his children,
And his eye fell on Sister Caroline,
Tossing on her bed of pain.
And God's big heart was touched with pity,
With the everlasting pity.
And God sat back on his throne,
And he commanded that tall, bright angel standing at his right hand:
Call me Death!
And that tall, bright angel cried in a voice
That broke like a clap of thunder:
Call Death!–Call Death!
And the echo sounded down the streets of heaven
Till it reached away back to that shadowy place,
Where Death waits with his pale, white horses.
And Death heard the summons,
And he leaped on his fastest horse,
Pale as a sheet in the moonlight.
Up the golden street Death galloped,
And the hooves of his horses struck fire from the gold,
But they didn't make no sound.
Up Death rode to the Great White Throne,
And waited for God's command.
And God said: Go down, Death, go down,
Go down to Savannah, Georgia,

Down in Yamacraw,
And find Sister Caroline.
She's borne the burden and heat of the day,
She's labored long in my vineyard,
And she's tired–
She's weary–
Go down, Death, and bring her to me.
And Death didn't say a word,
But he loosed the reins on his pale, white horse,
And he clamped the spurs to his bloodless sides,
And out and down he rode,
Through heaven's pearly gates,
Past suns and moons and stars;
on Death rode,
Leaving the lightning's flash behind;
Straight down he came.
While we were watching round her bed,
She turned her eyes and looked away,
She saw what we couldn't see;
She saw Old Death. She saw Old Death
Coming like a falling star.
But Death didn't frighten Sister Caroline;
He looked to her like a welcome friend.
And she whispered to us: I'm going home,
And she smiled and closed her eyes.
And Death took her up like a baby,
And she lay in his icy arms,
But she didn't feel no chill.
And death began to ride again–
Up beyond the evening star,
Into the glittering light of glory,
On to the Great White Throne.
And there he laid Sister Caroline
On the loving breast of Jesus.
And Jesus took his own hand and wiped away her tears,
And he smoothed the furrows from her face,

And the angels sang a little song,
And Jesus rocked her in his arms,
And kept a-saying: Take your rest,
Take your rest.
Weep not–weep not,
She is not dead;
She's resting in the bosom of Jesus.

Listen, Lord: A Prayer

O Lord, we come this morning
Knee-bowed and body-bent
Before Thy throne of grace.
O Lord--this morning--
Bow our hearts beneath our knees,
And our knees in some lonesome valley.
We come this morning--
Like empty pitchers to a full fountain,
With no merits of our own.
O Lord--open up a window of heaven,
And lean out far over the battlements of glory,
And listen this morning.

Lord, have mercy on proud and dying sinners--
Sinners hanging over the mouth of hell,
Who seem to love their distance well.
Lord--ride by this morning--
Mount Your milk-white horse,
And ride-a this morning--
And in Your ride, ride by old hell,
Ride by the dingy gates of hell,
And stop poor sinners in their headlong plunge.

And now, O Lord, this man of God,
Who breaks the bread of life this morning--
Shadow him in the hollow of Thy hand,
And keep him out of the gunshot of the devil.
Take him, Lord--this morning--
Wash him with hyssop inside and out,
Hang him up and drain him dry of sin.
Pin his ear to the wisdom-post,
And make his words sledge hammers of truth--
Beating on the iron heart of sin.
Lord God, this morning--

Put his eye to the telescope of eternity,
And let him look upon the paper walls of time.
Lord, turpentine his imagination,
Put perpetual motion in his arms,
Fill him full of the dynamite of Thy power,
Anoint him all over with the oil of Thy salvation,
And set his tongue on fire.

And now, O Lord--
When I've done drunk my last cup of sorrow--
When I've been called everything but a child of God--
When I'm done traveling up the rough side of the mountain--
O--Mary's Baby--
When I start down the steep and slippery steps of death--
When this old world begins to rock beneath my feet--
Lower me to my dusty grave in peace
To wait for that great gittin'-up morning--Amen.

John Andrew Schreiner

"Peace!"

Meditation on Paradise (Ode 11)

My heart was pruned and its flower appeared,
then grace sprang up within,
and my heart brought forth fruits in abundance for the Lord.
The Most High opened my heart towards Him, and filled me with His love.
and I ran in the Way, in His peace,
and I ran in the way of His truth
He took me to His Paradise
Where I beheld these trees
Whose branches were sprouting and full of fruits
Immortal land held their roots. A river of gladness watered them, And the land of eternal life.
And I said, Blessed, O Lord, are they who are planted in Your land,
Blessed, O Lord, are they who have a place in Your Paradise;
And the Lord is like the sun upon the face of the land
and I become the land that blossoms and rejoices in the light
Glory be to You, O God, the delight of Paradise for ever

I Have Been Freed

I have been freed, I am not condemned
(Bless the Lord O my Soul)
I have been freed; I am not condemned
(His mercy endures forever)
I went after truth and wandered not.
And the thought of truth led me and I wandered not.
And all who saw me were amazed,
and I seemed to them a stranger.
And I was justified by my Lord,
with Salvation that is pure forever.
I have been freed, I am not condemned
(Bless the Lord O my Soul)
I have been freed; I am not condemned
(His mercy endures forever)
He who knew me and raised me up,
is Messiah in all of His perfection.
He gave me a crown that was living
and showed me the way of His steps,
And I was justified by my Lord,
with Salvation that is pure forever.
I have been freed, I am not condemned
(Bless the Lord O my Soul)
I have been freed, I am not condemned
(His mercy endures forever)
My chains were cut off by His hands,
Glory to You Glory to You
I received the newness of life
Glory to You Glory to You
And He shattered the bars of iron,
Glory to You Glory to You
for my shackles had melted away
Glory to You Glory to You
Glory to You, Messiah.

Glory to You Our God
Glory to You, Messiah.
Glory to You Our God
I have been freed, I am not condemned
(Bless the Lord O my Soul)
I have been freed, I am not condemned
(His mercy endures forever)

I Shall Not Fear (Ode 5)

Because the Lord is my salvation
I will not fear
Because my confidence is in You
I will not fear
Because You are with me
I will not fear
For I am with You
Hallelujah, Hallelujah, Hallelujah, Hallelujah,
Amen

He blesses his people with peace (Ode 9)

Open our ears to hear You speak ,
The LORD gives strength to his people;
Your word and Your good pleasures,
He blesses his people with peace.
In Your will is our salvation,
The LORD gives strength to his people;
And Your thoughts are everlasting ,
He blesses his people with peace.

Be strong Be strong
and be redeemed and be redeemed
by His grace by His grace
Be strong Be strong
And receive. and receive
the gift of peace, the gift of peace

For you proclaim peace to your saints,
The LORD gives strength to his people;
those who receive, do not be ashamed,
He blesses his people with peace.
An everlasting crown is Truth,
The LORD gives strength to his people;
Blessed are they who wear it,
.He blesses his people with peace.
Open our ears to hear You speak ,
The LORD gives strength to his people;
Your word and Your good pleasures,
He blesses his people with peace.
In Your will is our salvation,
The LORD gives strength to his people;
And Your thoughts are everlasting ,
He blesses his people with peace.

Be strong Be strong

and be redeemed and be redeemed
by His grace by His grace
Be strong Be strong
And receive. and receive
the gift of peace, the gift of peace

For you proclaim peace to your saints,
The LORD gives strength to his people;
those who receive, do not be ashamed,
He blesses his people with peace.
An everlasting crown is Truth,
The LORD gives strength to his people;
Blessed are they who wear it, .
He blesses his people with peace.

A Cloud of Peace (Ode 35)

A cloud of peace has risen
Over my head
A cloud of peace has risen
over my head
My salvation
My salvation
A cloud of peace has risen
over my head

A cloud of peace has risen
Above my head

My salvation
My salvation

Eddy Duhan

"Unity!"

Creation Song

He wraps Himself in light
As with a garment
He spreads out the heavens
And walks on the wings of the wind.

He sends forth the springs
From the valleys
They flow between mountains.
The birds of the air dwell
By the waters,
Lifting their voices in song

Singing glory, glory!
Glory to the Lamb!
All praises and honor forever.

He made the moon for its seasons,
The sun knows its setting.
He looks at the Earth and it trembles,
He touches the mountains
And they smoke.

I will sing to the Lord all my life,
I will sing praises to my God
As long as I live,
Praises to the Lord, oh my soul.

I will Wait for my Change to Come

Man is born of woman,
His days are few, and full of trouble;
He springs up like a flower and withers
And disappears like a fleeing shadow.

If only You would hide me in the grave,
Conceal me until Your anger has passed;
Then I will answer You when You call my name,
When You long for the one Your hands have made.

All the days of my struggle
I will wait for my change,
I will wait for my change to come.
Only do not hide Your face from me,
Don't take Your hand away,
Don't take Your hand away.
I will wait for my change to come.

From the dust You have made me,
And to the dust I will return.
Surely You will count all my steps,
But will not keep watch for my sin.

The falling mountains crumble away,
The water ears away the stones.
Its torrents wash away the dust of the earth.
Only in You will I hope

Lamentation

How lonely lies the city,
Once so full of people.
Bitterly she weeps,
Tears upon her cheeks
Among all her lovers
There's no one left;
To comfort her,
Her friends became her enemies
They have all betrayed her.

I am a man who has seen affliction,
Streams of tears flow from my eyes,
He has driven me away in darkness,
Turned his hand against me again and again.

I called upon your name, O Lord,
Do not close your ears.
You came near when I called to you,
And you said, "Do not fear".

Let Light Shine

Let light shine out of darkness
For we have this treasure in earthen jars
To show his all surpassing power
Who makes his light shine in our hearts

We are hard pressed on every side
Perplexed but not in despair
Persecuted but not abandonded
Struck down but we rise again

Therefore let us not lose heart
Although we are wasting away
Inside we are being renewed day by day
We commend ourselves in every way
In great endurance in troubles
In hardships and distress
In sleepless nights and hunger
In purity, understanding, patience, and kindness.

Now if this earthly house we live in
Is torn down
We have a building from God
A house not made with human hands
Eternal in the heavens

Let light shine out of darkness

Treasures in Heaven

All flesh is like grass
And its loveliness like flower of the field
The grass withers and the flower fade
When the glory of the Lord shall be revealed

Lay up for yourselves treasures in heaven
Where moth and rust cannot destroy
For where your treasure is your heart will be
In the everlasting city of eternal joy

If you lay treasures on earth
Then thieves can come to break in and steal
And all its glory shall wear away
And the sky will be rolled up like a scroll

A crown of glory
An eternal home
No more sorrow
Never alone
With myriads of angels
Gathered at the throne

Treasures in heaven
Where moth and rust cannot destroy
Your heart will be
In the everlasting city of eternal joy

Song of Moses

The Lamb was standing on Mount Zion,
And I heard a voice from heaven,
Like the sound of many waters,
Like the sound of loud thunder.
Like the sound of harpists playing,
For those who had come victorious,
And they sang a new song before the throne,
And they sang the song of Moses!

Great and marvelous are your works!
Just and true are your ways.
Who will not fear who will not glorify your name,
For you alone are holy.

Sing to the Lord for He is highly exalted.
The horse and rider were hurled into the sea.
His right hand majestic in power,
His right hand shattered the enemy,
Let us rejoice let us rejoice and be glad!

Blessed are those who have come,
To the marriage supper of the Lamb,
For the bride has made herself ready,
Made herself ready.

Bible Prayers

Daniel prayed in the lion's den
Jonah prayed in the belly of the whale
Elijah prayed and the fire came down
Joshua prayed and the sun stood still

God be merciful to me a sinner
Not my will but Thine be done
Speak for your servant is listening
Here I am send me

Enoch prayed and he was no more
Noah prayed and God shut the door
Gideon prayed and he saw the sign
Samson prayed though his eyes were blind

And God delivered Job
When he prayed for his friends
And gave him twice as much
As he had in the end

The Lord said to my Lord

The Lord said to my Lord
The Lord said to my Lord
Sit at my right hand
Until your enemies are under your feet

The moon and sun will be darkened
The moon and sun will be darkened
The stars will fall from the heavens
Shaken by a mighty wind

He will send out his angels
He will send out his angels
And gather up all his elect
To the ends of heaven and earth

You will see the Son of Man
You will see the Son of Man
Seated at God's right hand
Coming with the clouds of heaven

Stand Up Michael!

Michael is sittin'
Sittin' in heaven
Waitin' for the Lord
To give the word
Saying stand up Michael
Michael stand up
And cast the devil
down to the world…

Listen God's children
And don't be fooled
If you're gonna be ready
You gotta be schooled
He prophesied it
In his word
When Satan pretends
To be the Lord…

Then Jesus will come
To gather his children
With all his angels
In flaming fire
The trumpet will sound
And awaken the dead
To eternity
Like John and Daniel said…

Daniel 12: ¹And at that time shall Michael stand up, the great prince which standeth for the children of thy people: and there shall be a time of trouble, such as never was since there was a nation even to that same time: and at that time thy people shall be delivered, every one that shall be found written in the book. (KJV)

Revelation 12: 7And there was war in heaven: Michael and his angels fought against the dragon; and the dragon fought and his angels, 8And prevailed not; neither was their place found any more in heaven. 9And the great dragon was cast out, that old serpent, called the Devil, and Satan, which deceiveth the whole world: he was cast out into the earth, and his angels were cast out with him. 10And I heard a loud voice saying in heaven, Now is come salvation, and strength, and the kingdom of our God, and the power of his Christ: for the accuser of our brethren is cast down, which accused them before our God day and night. 11And they overcame him by the blood of the Lamb, and by the word of their testimony; and they loved not their lives unto the death. 12Therefore rejoice, ye heavens, and ye that dwell in them. Woe to the inhabiters of the earth and of the sea! for the devil is come down unto you, having great wrath, because he knoweth that he hath but a short time. (KJV)

Photo by Jan Duhan

Eddy Duhan was born in the Long Lake district of Sudbury, Ontario Canada in 1954. He was the youngest of 5 children. His father died when he was 3 years old, so his family moved to North Battleford, Saskatchewan where Eddy was raised in the Roman Catholic, and Ukrainian Orthodox Catholic church's. In 1969 he had a life changing personal encounter with Christ at the beginning of the Jesus movement in Vancouver at the House of Daniel. He began writing poetry and music at age 15. Eddy eventually moved to Orange County California in the 1980's, and resides in Anaheim with his wife, and daughter. They attend St. John's Lutheran Church in the historic Old Town Orange.

Copyright 2012 Long Lake Publishing
ISBN 978-0982905944

www.ingramcontent.com/pod-product-compliance
Lightning Source LLC
Chambersburg PA
CBHW071500040426
42444CB00008B/1427